Praise for
The Monk of
Park Avenue

A wonderful tale of extortion, revenge, and love: a fast-paced rip-roaring race that will ignite almost every emotion you can imagine (and several you probably can't).

—GRAEME MAXTON, climate economist, activist, and former secretary general of the Club of Rome

"*The Monk of Park Avenue* is a compelling, sometimes disturbing—yet ultimately inspiring—memoir of one man's quest to transcend the disfunctions of his privileged Manhattan upbringing and America's obsessions with fame, power, and wealth by pursuing his childhood fascination with Chinese martial arts and the Daoist philosophy beneath it. Step-by-step, struggle-by-struggle, moving from one mentor to another, he finally meets a teacher who will take him into the deeper realms of Daoism, a foundational worldview extremely relevant in today's troubled world. This well-rendered, page-turning account is rich with timeless lessons and insights that Westerners would do well to pay attention to."

—TOM PEEK, author of the award winning novel *Daughters of Fire*

"Evokes a peek into a New York long gone but familiar right from the start, and then proceeds, with surprising speed, into a unique and inspiring journey most people can only dream about. A great read."

—PETER THOMAS ROTH, skin-care magnate

"If I was his Daoist abbot, I would have given Arthur Rosenfeld the monk name *Lei Ji* (Lightning Strike) instead of *Yun Rou* (Soft Cloud) as each page of the monk's memoir crackles with his lightning wit and enlightened observations that ripple forth from an electric mind. The first-born of a world-renowned cardiologist from the Upper East Side of Manhattan, young Arthur's life would appear to be one of great privilege—were it not for the abusive nanny who leaves no marks when she hits him or the school bullies who regularly chase after the weak, asthmatic boy to steal whatever money he has in his pockets before he can reach his home on Park Avenue. These early 'motivations' shape Arthur to defend the defenseless and give voice to the unheard through two yin yang arts: fighting and writing. As Arthur the incomparable martial artist-storyteller gives way to Yun Rou the spiritual philosopher-monk, his deep resolve to be a man of peace at all costs will be tested to the core when an invisible adversary incapacitates him and pushes him to the brink of death.

"*The Monk on Park Avenue* is much more than a memoir. As relentless and exhilarating as a waterfall, it seduces us into action to save our planet and fight the worthy fight—for our own sake, if not for future generations."

—DAISY LEE, founder of Radiant Lotus Qigong

"*The Monk of Park Avenue* is a beautiful story of a life well-lived amidst tragedies and triumphs, love and loss. From an early life of privilege among celebrities and society's elite to facing his own mortality in the jungles of Paraguay and jails of Ecuador, from facing down martial arts mobsters to confronting crooked corporate CEOs, Yun Rou's spiritual quest is one we can all relate to: seeking (and finding) balance in a topsy-turvy world. Highly Recommended."

—GREGORY RIPLEY, author of *Tao of Sustainability*

"Whatever you are doing, finish it before starting to read this book. Because this book will completely absorb your attention from the beginning, and you won't be able to focus on anything else. From the first page, you will have the impression of not only being in the hospital with this very sick two-year-old child, but inside him, in his feverish body. This is the exciting story of an unusual monk, decidedly different from the classical monk you have in your mind, the story of a physical and spiritual journey. It is a wonderful story, moving and entertaining, written in a visceral and limpid prose, by a truly great writer."

—EMANUELE PETTENER, PhD, assistant professor of Italian and writer in residence at Florida Atlantic University

"In his scintillating memoir, *The Monk of Park Avenue*, Daoist Monk Yun Rou sets forth the circuitous path by which the privileged son of a famous Manhattan doctor was transformed into a Chinese-ordained monk. In elegant writing that twists and tangles readers along the hairpin-turn trajectory of his fascinating and sometimes agonizing life, Yun Rou offers insight into martial arts, Hollywood, Daoism, writing, the meaning of life, and why one might want to learn how to hurl a giant spear. Entertaining, heartbreaking, and insightful by turns, his account explores the journey of someone driven from a young age to break his self-destructive patterns and become a force to serve and heal the world."

—NITA SWEENEY, certified meditation leader and award-winning author of *Depression Hates a Moving Target* and *Make Every Move a Meditation*

PRAISE FOR
THE MAD MONK
MANIFESTO

"Monk Yun Rou's new book, Mad Monk Manifesto—A *Prescription for Evolution, Revolution, and Global Awakening*, is a Taoist call to action to anyone wishing to save themselves and the planet."
—DANIELLE BOLELLI, PhD, author, professor, and host of *History on Fire* and *Drunken Taoist* podcasts

"In this wide ranging, amusing and thoughtful book *Mad Monk Manifesto—A Prescription for Evolution, Revolution, and Global Awakening*, Taoist Monk Yun Rou offers us a vision that can give hope to millions. It is a vision which is rooted in compassion, simplicity, and selflessness and offers a pathway to a sustainable world—not just spiritually—but practically too. It is a book for snacking but devouring too."
—GRAEME MAXTON, Secretary General of the Club of Rome and author of the bestselling books *The End of Progress* and *Reinventing Prosperity*

"With *Mad Monk Manifesto—A Prescription for Evolution, Revolution, and Global Awakening*, Monk Yun Rou presents a utopian treatise that reminds us of what we can aspire to. He has much wisdom to share."
—Dr. CARL PILCHER, PhD, Blue Marble Space Institute of Science, NASA (retired)

"Uplifting, inquisitive, and elegant in its delivery, Monk Yun Rou's newest work Mad Monk Manifesto—A Prescription for Evolution, Revolution, and Global Awakening shines a light on the importance of curiosity, kindness, and transformation in a world beset by overconsumption, the glorification of violence and the relentless inundation and demands of the Information Age. A wonderful read for anyone looking to gain perspective or insight on the power of simplification and wonder!"

—SARAH FIMM, American singer-songwriter residing in Woodstock, NY

Praise for Monk Yun Rou's other Books

Turtle Planet

"Turtles have been a part of Earth's natural balance for hundreds of millions of years. Now, human greed and indifference bring them to the very brink of extinction. In this passionate, shining work, Yun Rou champions their cause and indicts our self-destructive relationship with Mother Earth."

—William Holmstrom, Wildlife Conservation Society

"This beautiful, imaginative, and important work reminds us that turtles, unchanged for 200 million years, have been a cornerstone of folklore and religion since before recorded history. If we can come to see the threats facing them today, as Yun Rou has done here, then we can begin to repair what we have done."

—Anthony Pierlioni, Vice President and Senior Director, theTurtleRoom

A Cure for Gravity

"[A] charming tale.... There's a bravura innocence at the heart of this offbeat novel."

—*Publisher's Weekly*

"A touching ghost story that eludes easy comparison to any other book. An amazing, rewarding voyage.... No need to imitate other writers; Rosenfeld is a true original."
—*Booklist*

"A zesty, comic, high-speed American gothic."
—*Kirkus Reviews*

"*A Cure for Gravity* is the kind of stunning surprise that comes along once a year, if we're lucky. It's like expecting a ninety-dollar bicycle for Christmas, and getting a brand new Harley instead.... It will be the rare reader who turns the last page without a lump in his throat and a smile on his lips."
—*Florida Sun Sentinel*

"[An] unusual yarn [that] intrigues and grips...doesn't let up until the last page."
—Barbara Taylor Bradford, *New York Times* bestselling author

"This wonderful novel doesn't just cure gravity, it cures all matters of heart, mind, and soul. I felt better after reading the title alone; imagine how I felt after reading the whole book."
—Neil Simon, Pulitzer Prize winning playwright of *The Odd Couple*, *Lost in Yonkers*, and more

"Rosenfeld uses the tangle of lives he has created to tell a story that has its mystical moments—but is every bit about the needs of the living. This makes it a love story, of course, and a sweet, telling one at that."
—*The New York Daily News*

"A *Cure for Gravity* may be seen as mainstream fiction that just happens to be fast, funny, outrageous, and full of heart."

—*The Mercury News*, San Jose, CA

"A Cure for Gravity roars along at the pace of an open throttled motorcycle."

—*The Tribune*, South Bend, IN

"With A *Cure for Gravity*, Mr. Rosenfeld inspires the deepest emotion one writer can feel about another: envy."

—Larry Gelbart, creator of *M*A*S*H*, *Tootsie*, *A Funny Thing Happened on the Way to the Forum*, and more

"A novel of surprising imagination and stylistic daring....A *Cure for Gravity* rises to near greatness as a piece of home-grown Magical Realism. Touching, scary, hilarious."

—Knight Ridder News Service

"This book is like reading a story and listening to music at the same time. A page-turner with rhythm, and a most unusual narrative voice. I loved the characters, the views of an America I haven't seen, the unexpected twists and turns. A wonderful book."

—Jack Paar, former host of *The Tonight Show*

"Arthur Rosenfeld's A *Cure for Gravity* is a noir mystery, a supernatural thriller, a crime caper novel, a love story, and an American road-trip adventure—all seamlessly woven into one moving, magical book. If the ghosts of Jack Kerouac and Jim Thompson could collaborate with Alice Hoffman, this is the story they might write.... This novel twists, spins, and rages like an Oklahoma tornado, and it'll fling you up into the

cruel sky before bringing you back down to the good earth...
safe, but shaken. Hell, it'll make you fly."

Diamond Eye

"This is, to put it bluntly, one of the freshest, most enjoyable
mysteries to come along in the last couple of years.... Any
novel that features people with names like Seagrave Chunny,
Phayle Tollard, and Twy Boatright is a novel that practically
demands to be read.... The plot is delightfully twisty, turny,
and, at times, surprisingly thought provoking."

"A great read in the noir tradition."

"*Diamond Eye* is a special delivery, no doubt about that.
Refreshingly different. With its wit, warmth, and
wonderfully wild cast, Rosenfeld dexterously blends
cinematic scenes with intricate, often humorous personality
studies in what may be this year's most promising detective
series introduction. Hey, who knew that detective fiction
could benefit from going postal?"

"Rosenfeld writes a muscular prose that moves along at a
brisk clip."

"Exploring cop-struggling-against-criminal-desire themes hauntingly reminiscent of Hammett's *Red Harvest*, Rosenfeld crafts a high-action suspense thriller with plenty of wry humor and cultural commentary."
—*Publisher's Weekly*

"Rosenfeld's likeable detective has a genuine disgust for the felons that he pursues and the determination necessary to bring them to justice."
—*The Dallas Morning News*

"Rosenfeld skillfully weaves a complex plot that defies solution until the very last pages. In the process, he creates an urbane, life-loving, self-effacing, and courageous character who should forever dispel the erroneous image of 'lowly' postal inspectors."
—*The Boca Raton/Delray Beach News*

"Rosenfeld keeps things moving smartly even before the nifty twist that ties his two plots together into a neat, grisly bow."
—*Kirkus Reviews*

The Cutting Season

"Arthur Rosenfeld's *The Cutting Season* is a marvelously entertaining blend of many different genres: medical thriller, psychological suspense, fantasy, martial arts adventure, romance, and crime drama, all neatly packaged into three hundred engrossing pages."
—Mostlyfiction.com

"...an intriguing premise as the hero rationalizes his vigilante justice... to do nothing would be amoral. Fascinating."
—*The Midwest Book Review*

"Remarkable!...a literary masterpiece...exceptionally well-paced and hard to put down...unique insights in the mysterious world of classical martial arts."
—Lawrence Kane, author of *Surviving Armed Assaults*

The Crocodile and the Crane

"Arthur Rosenfeld has done it again!"
—*Virginia Gazette*

"...a thriller of uncommon inventiveness. In the hand of the right filmmaker, *The Crocodile and the Crane* could be a terrific movie."
—*Florida Sun-Sentinel*

Tai Chi: The Perfect Exercise

"In *Tai Chi: The Perfect Exercise*, Arthur Rosenfeld draws from modern newsfeeds and a multitude of personal colorful anecdotes to illuminate this time-honored art. He brings a charmingly refreshing voice to the study and practice of Tai Chi."
—Gene Ching, associate publisher of *Kung Fu Tai Chi* magazine & KungFuMagazine.com

"Arthur Rosenfeld has written the most accessible book on Tai Chi I've seen. Its benefits are scientifically proven, and I'll be recommending this to my patients young and old."

— Mark Lachs, MD, MPH, professor of medicine, Weill Cornell Medical College

"Rosenfeld's book will improve your health and your mind. Easy and fun to read, it is filled with uplifting stories, lots to make you think about the world and plenty of easy-to-follow practical fitness advice. A delight."

— Graeme Maxton, bestselling author and fellow of the Club of Rome

"After my own decades of attempting to convey in ordinary English the deep and subtle insights of the Taoist traditions, I can appreciate the masterful contribution Arthur Rosenfeld had made with his *Tai Chi: The Perfect Exercise*. He brings sharp clarity to a subject too often shrouded in mystery and confusion."

— Guy Leekley, author of *Tao Te Ching: A New Version for All Seekers*

"Arthur Rosenfeld is one of the most special and genuine voices in the arts today. Not persuaded by fame, attention, or self-congratulatory actions, he walks a path that is unique, winding, and full of discoveries, surprises, and truth, not just for himself but for those lucky enough to align themselves with him."

— Del Weston, martial artist, producer, writer and director

"Arthur Rosenfeld is rightfully one of the foremost Tai Chi masters in this country if not the world. This mastery has spiraled into his writing. This book has illumined my Tai Chi practice. It also offered fresh teaching examples in the areas of breath and energy that I can share with my students. I'm highly appreciative of his contribution with this book."

—Mitchell Doshin Cantor, Sensei of The Southern Palm Zen Group

"Arthur Rosenfeld's new book, Tai Chi: The Perfect Exercise, breathes new life into the old saying bun bu ichi (the ways of the sword and those of the pen are one). It's extremely rare to find a martial artist whose practical expertise and martial insight are paired with literary elegance, enthusiasm, and rich experience.... Lucidly organized, elegantly written and filled with the types of insights that are only too rare in this genre.... The author's mastery of clear and accomplished prose...make this a valuable and mature meditation on the virtually limitless depths of this art."

—John Donahue, bestselling author of Enzan

"Rosenfeld's Tai Chi is as unique a contribution to the martial art as Bruce Lee's Tao of Jeet Kune Do was to his. This muscular work weaves history and modernity with philosophy and combat to create a tapestry that transcends all disciplines. Tai Chi will travel with you regardless of where you go and regardless of whether you take it."

—Cameron Conaway, author of Caged: Memoirs of a Cage-Fighting Poet

THE
MONK
OF
PARK AVENUE

THE
MONK
OF
PARK AVENUE

A Modern Daoist Odyssey

YUN ROU

mango
PUBLISHING
CORAL GABLES

Cover Design: Roberto Nuñez
Layout & Design: Carmen Fortunato

For permission requests, please contact the publisher at:
Mango Publishing Group
2850 S Douglas Road, 4th Floor
Coral Gables, FL 33134 USA
info@mango.bz

For special orders, quantity sales, course adoptions and corporate
sales, please email the publisher at sales@mango.bz. For trade
and wholesale sales, please contact Ingram Publisher Services at
customer.service@ingramcontent.com or +1.800.509.4887.

The Monk of Park Avenue: A Modern Daoist Odyssey

Library of Congress Cataloging-in-Publication number: 2022931109
ISBN: (print) 978-1-64250-608-2, (ebook) 978-1-64250-609-9
BISAC category code PHI023000, PHILOSOPHY / Taoist

Printed in the United States of America

CONTENTS

FOREWORD

How does a monk come to write a memoir? Aren't monks and nuns about quiet, selfless service, banished egos, and contemplative lives? Should not such a person be entirely and exclusively engaged in rituals, devotions, and practices? When not meditation or praying, should not such a person be planting seeds in a garden and helping the hungry, homeless, or afflicted rather than doing any kind of work that draws attention? I tend to think the answer is yes. My masters have both made it clear that there are many ways to be of service, and that both writing and teaching are well-recognized in the monastic tradition. In any case, as much as I love to be out and about in the mountains, I'm better with a keyboard than I am digging for herbs.

The world has changed a great deal since the sages of old taught small groups of followers or brush-stroked their wisdom onto scrolls. While I am no sage master, I do recognize that whether we are billionaires or homeless dumpster divers, our personal narratives define us just as the narratives of culture, community, and nation-states define the politics of the human world. Lessons and ideas, it turns out, are most easily relatable, memorable, and understandable when they are presented in narrative form.

My own story, this memoir, starts on the dazzling streets of Manhattan living a life that for most people would be the stuff of fantasy. Moving from that privileged milieu to an original and unique path of love, loss, pain, battles, lightning bolts from out of the blue, and, perhaps most significantly, my own death, I finally arrive at a place of harmony and balance

I scarcely dared imagine I would ever find. Sharing that path here gives context to my beliefs. It illuminates how and why I have come to believe that Daoism, an ancient, shamanic-based philosophy and religion, holds the key to restoring peace, health, harmony, and balance to the world and that its precepts and practices can be of great use in making each of our lives less stressful, less of a struggle, more loving, frugal, humble, and perhaps most of all, more compassionate.

One last note: there are some places where I have manipulated the timeline to make the read smoother and easier to follow. For example, there is a section where I describe reading a copy of *The Tibetan Book of Living and Dying*. The details are correct, but I actually read that book during another, later, cross-country sojourn. It had not yet been published at the time of the first ride. I conflated the two adventures because this is not a motorcycle memoir, and I didn't want to burden the reader with more detail than needed to tell the story and get the point across. There may be a handful of other similar instances, but in a world where memoirists are occasionally accused of blurring the lines between fact and fiction, I can only say that human memory is fallible. Dates and details aside, everything chronicled below actually occurred. Some names have been changed to protect individuals' privacy. Because the narrative goes back more than half a century, political correctness may not be in evidence—particularly in the early chapters—because I am indeed telling it as it was. The world in which I write this memoir is a world wracked by dizzyingly fast change. With any luck, the reader will indulge me that and be able to see the growth and trajectory in my own view of the world.

That is, of course, the whole point. I only wish my late father were here to read what follows.

CHAPTER 1

SPONGE IN A HURRICANE

M y birth name is Arthur Rosenfeld, and the year is 1959. I'm two years old, and I spike such a fever that my father is convinced I'm going to die of spinal meningitis. Other children with such symptoms are given sponge baths and Tylenol—now known to kill the liver in even modest doses—but because my father is a soon-to-be world-famous cardiologist, I'm rushed to the hospital and laid out, naked and face down, on a metal table. My bare chest, belly, and thighs pucker against the cold surface and my budding manhood shrinks. I cry and scream and soon discover what all fighting arts teach, namely that I'm stronger contracting than expanding.

It takes four full-sized adults to restrain me while a doctor, prognosticating darkly, presses a long, thick needle into the meat of my spine and extracts from it, without anesthesia, a measure of fluid, precious and clear. My position gives me a one-eyed view of the world during this procedure. I see my father's agonized expression. I see tall, green, paint-chipped bottles of oxygen. I see lots of white shoes and a stainless-steel cart on wheels bearing a tray that bristles with syringes, clamps, and gauze pads. I see the broad, scrubbed fingernails and extruding forearm tendons of the men leaning heavily on my limbs.

It later emerges that I'm not going to die but merely have the flu. To this day, I remain sore at the spot of that needle's entry, though that soreness may be no more than the sort of rebellious phantom that plagues an amputee home from war. I believe its lifelong presence then kindled, and now feeds, a strong empathetic kinship with the forced, helpless, and oppressed. That needle set the stage for a certain vigilance robustly hardwiring my brain for self-preservation. The moment that needle was forced into me, I became a compassionate warrior.

I might have come to compassion even without the trauma, given that it runs in my family of doctors. A couple of years after the spinal tap, when I'm four and watching my Jewish father perform what is for him the holiest of holy religious rituals—the swapping of a heavy overcoat for the white one awaiting him in the Doctor's Coat Room at New York Hospital. This somber, sacred, and self-congratulatory donning is performed in the company of other men who also wear shirts, ties, and stethoscopes, the latter usually slung around their necks, though my father's is looped and stuffed into his coat pocket. My father tells me that he has waited a long time to bring me into this inner *sanctum*.

Preparing to sally forth in the vestments of hope, godliness, and power, he tells me to wait patiently for him as he saves lives. I perch on a dusty, overstuffed couch positioned between faux Tiffany lamps and employ crayons and a coloring book in my battle with the excruciatingly slow passage of time. The carriage clock on the mantelpiece ticks loudly. I look up expectantly each time the door opens, but despite the number of doctors coming and going, I do not see my father. In fact, he is gone for hours. During this interlude, and indeed during the rest of my childhood, I, the son of an anointed man, construe that I'm in training to be anointed myself. I close my eyes and imagine the early priests of my inherited faith dispatching judgment and decrees on Jerusalem's Temple Mount. I see these divine interlocutors wearing not white coats but white robes, as that is the way they are rendered in a children's book about the Bible that my mother, Camilla, a student of both philosophy and religion, has given me.

There is no evidence of the organic world of which doctors and patients alike are a part of in this coatroom, and there is certainly no hint of the frogs, turtles, halberds, spears, swords, jungle plants, bearded monks, and snow-capped Chinese peaks that will, years from now, be the trappings of my own path to service. Everything is cold and clinical here even though the building's heating pipes click and pop with contained steam. Despite some of the best of intentions, this is a world built on the hubris of men, a castle built to wall off our entire species from the rest of the world, for doctors have been told—biblically, not just in medical school—that they have dominion over all. No women are in evidence.

My father returns and we make our way to the hospital garage and his pea-soup-green Plymouth. When it becomes clear we are not heading home, he tells me that we must make a house call because someone's heart is sick. He says I will have to wait in the car, or maybe, if the patient is stable, in the kitchen. Somewhere along Manhattan's East River, he stops short to avoid rear-ending the car in front of us and I'm propelled face-first into the metal dashboard. I'm sucking my thumb at the time, wearing a deerstalker cap and a camel-colored car coat with broad tortoise-shell buttons. I bite the flesh of that thumb, bruise my teeth, get a swollen forehead, and cry, as much from surprise as pain. Looking stricken, my father jams the gearshift lever into park and leans in to tend me. The car rocks back and forth as the transmission protests such rough treatment. Seeing my father so worried, I resolve to protect him so he can continue being a god. I understand that my father and I are taking care of each other. Somehow, I know that it's a formative moment. This kind of knowing, I dimly realize, is not very common for kids my age.

I have just begun to meet such kids at a school called Dalton, which is housed in a big building on East 89th Street between Lexington and Park Avenues, a bit west of our apartment on East End Avenue. My Dalton classroom smells of chalk, the sweetness of lunchbox fruit, and the sweat of my teacher's armpits. The teacher's name is Ms. B. She has blonde hair tied up in a bun and I think she is pretty. I don't realize at the time that she sweats because she is nervous. She helps me learn to write, and I find that I like block letters better than script (now called cursive) because block letters are clearer. With block letters, everyone knows exactly what you mean. I express this preference out loud and the whole room grows quiet. Ms. B has no counter for it, so thereafter I'm allowed to add sharp edges to my letters while others are encouraged to flow. This feels like a victory to me—a triumph of individuation and rationalization in a world that seems increasingly arbitrary and more about convention and tradition than personal expression or common sense. Adding clear ends and edges also allows me to slow things down.

Right from the start, it seems to me that everyone and everything moves too fast at school. I suppose I feel this about life in general, but particularly when it comes to studying and learning I wonder why everything feels so rushed. Everyone else wants to move horizontally toward some set goal or end, ticking off subjects on a list before really understanding them, while I want to move vertically and let ideas percolate. In kindergarten and grade school I'm less concerned with memorizing facts than I am with cultivating a sense of wonder and pleasure in learning. Later, I discover that many of the facts I've been taught will need to be updated, completely discarded, and often replaced. As early as grade school, if not kindergarten, I realize that details and memorization are far less important to me than principles. I'm a Big Picture kind of kid.

At home, my brother, Stephen, turns two. He is my only sibling at the time and sleeps in a crib. I ask my mother to pull Stephen's crib closer to my junior bed so we can play together through the bars. One night, in the wash of a little yellow nightlight shaped like a seashell, I move Stephen's crib by myself. This requires me to brace my heels against the wall and use my upper body and my legs. I find this initial discovery of physical strength exhilarating. Encased in a baby blue, rabbit-style onesie that buttons in the front all the way from throat to diaper, Stephen watches me with his big dark eyes, his infant hands on the bars of his crib. When the move is complete, I want him to play in the bed with me but find I can't quite lift him out of the crib. Instead, I beckon for him to climb.

You can do it.

I tell him as his bootie-clad feet slide against the bars and smooth, tiny hands struggle at the bars of the crib. I keep encouraging him, he keeps trying, and eventually he summits. Perched on the thin railing, he gurgles and coos. My mother hears what passes as our conversation and bursts into the room to find Stephen about to tumble and me beckoning, a mischievous grin on my face.

She dashes in, rescues Stephen, cuddles him, and slaps me hard.

What do you think you're doing?

I tell her that I'm trying to get Stephen into bed with me so we can play together. She is having none of this prosaic and truthful explanation. Her look makes it clear that I have just revealed myself as an evil mastermind, an incarnate devil whose work in the world is her mission to counter. From that moment forward she is suspicious of any request or plan I might have. What satanic agenda, for instance, might be the true motivation behind my request for chocolate cereal? Why am I *really* interested in wearing striped shorts? Might it be because deep down I know I'll be incarcerated in a rural prison someday? Looking back, I realize she was just a woman in her early twenties married to a tornado of a career man. Feeling out of control despite being an ardent devotee of Jewish philosopher Martin Buber, she is at sea and searching for a mooring, desperately in need of a script to help her play the role of wife and mother. Her role as protagonist is apparently helped by the presence of an adversary.

The battle lines drawn, my mother and I develop our strategic alliances. I make a focused effort to enlist my father against her. Since he is rarely home, this proves to be a challenge. She, in turn, enlists our newly hired nanny,

Siegfried, as her confederate. Siegfried is a tall German woman with close-cropped dark hair. Upon hearing the news that I'm a scheming manipulator with a destructive agenda, Siegfried responds that Stephen, by contrast, is an absolute angel. My mother clearly agrees.

My treatment at Siegfried's hands is not pretty. Within range of my always-preoccupied mother, she is firm but fair. Firmer with me, of course, because I'm able to do more than just toddle around. Absent any witnesses, however, there is ice cream and hot chocolate for Stephen, but water for me. I accuse Siegfried of these discriminations, of course, as I'm rapidly developing a precocious sense of self-righteous injustice, but she merely laughs and tells my mother I have quite an imagination. Things continue this way, with Siegfried's slights against me gradually and progressively subtler and more pervasive. She never fails to bundle me against the cold, for example, as to do so would invite reprimand should I fall ill. With no one watching, however, there is nothing to stop her from gleefully buttoning my collar so tightly I can barely move or breathe. Near suffocation is difficult but it passes. What doesn't pass—what in fact takes root in the fertile soil of my mother's mind—is that I'm at least a storyteller and more likely a liar, someone wont to twist the truth rather than speak it. Indeed, I learn to find great succor in telling stories, particularly when simply stating the facts won't avail. It will be nearly half a century before I really own the power of storytelling—before I understand that without our stories, empty and alone, we simply disappear.

My miniature war with Siegfried has its vicissitudes but eventually comes to a close adjacent to Cleopatra's Needle in New York's Central Park. That's the day she beats me about the head—careful to leave no mark through my woolens—

and twists my fingers until I cry, causing a painful but invisible injury. Later, in martial arts class, I will learn how to do this better than she does. Fortunately for me, she is no kung fu master, and even more fortunately she is caught in the act by the wife of one of my father's colleagues. The woman makes a report to her husband, who then tells my father. Siegfried's departure leaves my mother temporarily forced to care for two children by herself. Facing that challenge, she takes the position that I might have told the truth once, but only as an exception to my usual stories and lies. Another nanny is soon in place but so is my conviction that I may as well play the part of the troublemaker. After all, I reason, if I'm paying for the crime, why not do it?

My mother is just following the path she knows. She's in a replay of her upper-class mother Hilda's marriage to an ambitious, up-and-coming physician, Arthur Master, after whom I am named. Grandpa Arthur grows up on the Lower East Side, goes to medical school, becomes a cardiologist, explores the idea that the human heart behaves differently under load than it does at rest, invents the precursor of today's treadmill, and finally marries the daughter—my grandmother.

Hilda is a kindly woman with a smoker's cough. She dies when I'm barely more than a toddler. Her sister, my Great Aunt Edith, steps into my life. She's married to Herbert Lehman, four-term governor of the State of New York, New York Senator, Director General of the United Nations Relief and Rehabilitation Administration, and early partner in the now-infamous Lehman Brothers banking firm. Early Lehman money is made off trading slave cotton. Herbert and Edith have three kids. One is adopted from Georgia Tann, a notorious child trafficker, whose black-market adoption scheme misleads many notable families between 1920 and 1950 before being shut down.

My parents, siblings, and I lunch on Sundays with Uncle Herbert and Aunt Edith at their Park Avenue duplex. We eat lambchops with paper handles, spooning green mint jelly onto the meat with silver spoons tucked into crystal bowls. We endure overcooked vegetables and slather everything with gravy. I sometimes sit next to Uncle Herbert and do my best to talk to him even though I am only six years old. Late in his life, in addition to much notable philanthropy and an enviable political record of effectiveness, honesty, and integrity, he is President John F. Kennedy's righthand man. Two days after Kennedy is shot, I'm beside Uncle Herbert while everyone eats quietly, trying to ignore the fact that the great man's bald head is resting on his plate and is not moving at all. Finally, while the rest of us are enjoying a dessert called Floating Island, he lifts his head and looks down the long table at his wife.

They shot JFK.

I know, dear.

I don't want to live in a world where people do such things.

I hear him say this, and on the way home from lunch, I tell my mother, in my little six-year-old voice, that I think Uncle Herbert is going to die. Two weeks later, dressing to receive the Presidential Medal of Freedom from President Lyndon Johnson, he drops dead in his bathroom.

Aunt Edith outlives him by thirteen years. During this time, she becomes a significant philanthropist in her own right. One utterly insignificant dimension of her philanthropy is to support my childhood interest in reptiles and amphibians, something she perhaps responds to because she and Uncle Herbert gave New York City a children's zoo in Central Park. To the horror of my parents, but with their great forbearance, I fill my room with lizards, snakes, turtles, salamanders, and frogs. I line them up in aquaria, which I painstakingly craft so that each is a window into a secret world of what I somehow sense is real and important.

I create tropical jungles here, replete with the snouts of lizards protruding from beneath curved pieces of wood and perfectly camouflaged chameleons moving in slow motion down the stalks of plants in pursuit of haplessly chirping crickets, their long, curled tongues waiting to unfold like sticky, red cinnamon rolls. I set up miniature indoor ponds, too, so that little swimming turtles can break water to listen to the music I play, which issues from loudspeakers powered by electronics bristling with vacuum tubes that glow red. Surrounding myself with the best I can get of nature is how I countervail all I keep being *told* is real, namely the arbitrary, concocted, imaginary, and artificial laws and worlds that the humans around me craft to insulate from their true selves.

Aunt Edith drives around in a black stretch limo with the license plate "L." Her chauffeur is known to the family only as "Smith," but he has a long history of driving the senator/governor and his wife. One day in the early '70s, Smith takes me, all by myself, down to a famous reptile store on West 14th Street called Fang and Claw. A legendary purveyor named Aldo Passera runs it, and has an amazing collection jammed into a small storefront. For the first time in the shop's history, the gubernatorial limousine pulls up to the front door. Aldo sells me an eastern indigo snake, which is now a protected species.

Aunt Edith's brother is Frank Altschul, a scion of investment banking—first in San Francisco and then in New York. Uncle Frank is a secret advisor to presidents, and as private a person as Uncle Herbert is public. A chess master and brilliant financier, he replaces his father in the early 1900s as a founding member of the banking house Lazard Freres, amassing a mighty personal fortune before founding Overbrook Management to manage the family money. He is one of the few Americans to ever be awarded the French Legion of Honor and serves as vice president and secretary of the Council on Foreign Relations, which publishes *Foreign Affairs* magazine. He runs the Overbrook Press, named for his farm, and through it publishes fine editions of collectible books. When he is already an old man, he stumbles on the stairs at Overbrook Farm, his Stamford, Connecticut estate, and puts out one of his eyes with the stem of his pipe. A glass one goes in but the real one leaves my mouth dry whenever he aims it at me. He is a powerful presence in our family, and perhaps the only person I have ever seen intimidate my father.

My father is, in turn, the one person who seems able to intimidate *me*. Sometime during fourth grade, I bring home the first of what will be many lackluster report cards. It is repeatedly said that I am not living up to my potential. Learning disabilities are largely unknown, and my teachers opine that because I can't sit still and am not riveted by their discourse, I am a lazy, unfocused daydreamer. Sitting behind his desk at our second Manhattan apartment at 90th Street and Park Avenue with a collection of Dunhill Briar and Meerschaum pipes behind him, my father interprets what these academic opinions bode for my future.

THE MONK OF PARK AVENUE

> With such poor grades, you will never become a doctor.
> You won't become a lawyer or even a captain of industry. If
> you're lucky, you will end up a doorman.

I love those pipes of his and just a few years later, in a show of sentimentality, I tell him I would like to have those pipes when he dies. My brother is there and adds that he would like to have our apartment.

Our building has a doorman, an Irishman named Eddy who happily helps by walking residents' dogs in the rain, delivering packages, and, of course, opening doors. His does not seem a bad lot but I wisely elect not to share this opinion with my father. Instead, I point at the bookshelves all around us, and then, in particular, at a copy of *Ivanhoe* by Sir Walter Scott, a fanciful depiction of medieval England, replete with chivalrous knights, robbers, and witches. I have been trying to read it, and though I find the language daunting, I'm engaged by the world Scott portrays and tell my father how I feel.

> The guy who wrote that book decides who lives and who
> dies. He decides who wins fights and who loses them, who
> marries whom, who gets rich and who stays poor. He's like
> God. I want his job. I want to be a writer and I think my
> daydreaming will help.

This distraction from my academic shortcomings renders my father momentarily speechless. In the rare silence that follows, I leave the room thinking not only of the story of Ivanhoe but of the plentiful tales right in my own family.

———·———

Then there is Grandpa Arthur's only son, also named Arthur, who graduates from Harvard with a degree in physics and starts a company to manufacture lightweight aerospace parts out of beryllium. The company takes off (no pun intended) and makes him a bundle. He's not big on commitment, so after he retires at the age of forty, he enjoys the company of many beautiful women. He's honest, compassionate, generous, and an overall prince of a guy. On account of his arcane intelligence and James Bond lifestyle, people in the family speculate he may secretly be a government spy. I call him Unk.

Unk has gray eyes, some shoulders and chin. Barrel-chested, he is a powerful man but too clumsy to be a real athlete. (Physical clumsiness runs in my family.) Unk is a bit socially awkward as well, but in a guileless, childish way that lets his beautiful heart shine through. He is the best uncle any kid could ever hope to have. With his retirement money, he buys an apartment on Sutton Place. The walls are covered in brown suede and framed prints of Helmut Newton photos, showing beautiful men and women dressed for social climbing. The bed has four chrome posts that match adjacent chrome sconces. There are stacks and stacks of *Playboy* magazine hiding below the bed frame. The balcony has a good view of the 59th Street Bridge, and Unk has parties there. One of them, years later, will be in celebration of my first published book.

Unk likes antique cars. He buys a couple in rough condition and restores them as a summertime hobby. One is a 1937 Mercedes 540K, a Nazi staff car with swoopy lines and a big engine. Another is a 1931 Phantom II Rolls Royce. I spend time outside of school working on that Rolls with him several summers in a row. We rebuild the engine together as well as the shock absorbers. He puts together a wood shop to manufacture a new ash wood frame for the rotted old trunk. As we work, he teaches me about things beyond internal combustion.

Cars like this were built to last forever. If the owners had taken better care, it would still be on the road. Very little is made that way anymore because people don't care. They don't take pride in craftsmanship and don't value durability. Our economy is built on disposing of things and buying new ones. Everything is about profit, even that great big last war of ours. Someone always makes a fortune when people start killing each other.

I want to know if it wasn't also about defeating the Nazis and the Japanese.

Unk regards me for a long moment before going back to work.

That too.

One night, Unk shows up at our Park Avenue apartment with a Super-8 movie projector and a portable projection screen. He knows how to work the thing, how to feed the film reel through the sprockets. My family, now with four children, includes Stephen, my sister, Hildi, and my youngest brother, Herbert, and we watch raptly as strange symbols appear on the screen, followed by a charismatic Chinese man, lean and muscled, whooping, grunting, whistling, and hooting as he kicks goons in the head and prances around with his shirt off. Unk and my father laugh, my mother leaves the room in disgust, but I'm fascinated.

What is this thing called kung fu?

My uncle laughs.

You're looking at it. Believe me when I tell you that if his exercises don't kill him, this guy Bruce Lee is going to be famous someday.

My toddler flu is not all that keeps me from becoming Bruce Lee. Unlike the soon-to-be-super-famous martial arts icon, I'm a chubby, slow-moving kid with bad lungs. I can't run and I don't know how to fight. The day after watching the film, I walk home from school and, as routinely happens, become street prey. Usually, being mugged involves no more than a one-on-one pushing and shoving, kicking, and punching before my money is taken. This time, there is a blade involved and a whole gang. Feeling the press of the cold steel in the small of my back as I'm relieved of a single dollar, I think about Bruce Lee's moves, and I think about my family being turned into lampshades and soap during Hitler's Holocaust. I wonder if my mother's hostility toward me has been put there for the purpose of training at least one fighter in a family that has lost so much.

The confluence of street crime and Bruce Lee's movies leads me to the TV show *Kung Fu*. The show's protagonist, a Chinese Shaolin monk named Kwai Chang Caine, expelled from his native land for killing an abusive nobleman, wanders the American West in search of his long-lost brother. In a perfect world, Bruce Lee would win this part and the show would showcase his talents. 1970's Hollywood, sadly, is not ready for an Asian leading man, so David Carradine stars. Carradine moves poorly but his portrayal of a monk's equanimity compels me to wonder what it might actually be like to be so calm and peaceful. Flashbacks to Caine's life in China also show his monk masters. One of them, blind Master

Po, can defeat all comers and hear a cricket break wind at a hundred yards. Swords and axes barely get a rise out of him, and he steps with perfection and grace, following his inner light. He is a man who understands the way the world really works. Watching the show, I want to blink and magically shed my limitations. I want to completely rewrite the myths and legends of my own life. I want to know what Master Po knows. I want an IV of that philosophy. As much as I envy Bruce Lee's charisma and athleticism, I don't want to be him. I want to be Po.

I take this quest as seriously as my twelve-year-old brain will allow. I understand that Po is at least a fiction and at most an archetype. Still, I believe he can sense the deepest levels of reality. Curious about Po's ethos, I delve deeply into the titles in my mother's philosophy library. Her collection is heavy in the area of Jewish and Western thought, but also offers select Asian titles. Trendy Zen Buddhist texts come first, and I find them suitably inscrutable but delicious. Daoist works, specifically the *Zhuangzi* and Laozi's *Daodejing,* follow. I love the crazy story-wisdom of the first and feel strangely moved by the second, as if it holds the secrets of the universe—if I could only understand it.

I don't have the same feeling about the education elsewhere in my life. So many of the tales I'm told by my parents and teachers and what is written in the newspaper seem somehow dubious to me. Nothing before me—not the rules of society, religion, politics, labels, race, social class, work, obligation, discipline, duty, or death—matches the simplicity of Po's days of devotion and practice and contemplation at the monastery. I sense something gritty and real about the natural world he is seeking to understand—eagles overhead, a turtle in hand, droughts and floods and autumn leaves and running streams—even though there seems so very little of any of that in life on Park Avenue. In rejecting the surface world around me in favor of what lies beneath, I feel alienated from friends and family alike.

Decades before *The Matrix*, this conviction that things are not as they seem grows by the day. Joe Frank—later of underground radio fame but now my writing teacher at Dalton—tries to convince me that it is art more than nature that reveals the truth below. Though young, Joe is already slightly grizzled, pockmarked, disaffected, and, like me, deeply dubious about elements of New York life. He admits that he often sits alone at his piano thinking dark thoughts. In class, he ruminates aloud on the dark revelations of Kafka and other literary giants. Despite loving the reading and writing I do in Joe's class, I'm driven to take a dentist's pick to everything I'm asked to accept, to make the gums of my own spirit ooze. There is simply so much distracting debris caught between my teeth, so much more truth I want from the world. When I reconnect with Joe decades later in Los Angeles, where his own dark visions fill the late-night airwaves, he tells me he is not surprised at what I have become. He avows that he saw the seed of the seeker in me back then, despite my apparent extroversion. He continues to contend that art is the final arbiter of truth. I smile, touch his shoulder, and tell him that each and every one of us is just a piece of nature, and what is truest in us is just nature's way of peeking through.

There is darkness in another of my high school teachers at Dalton, though I won't really learn of it until he is revealed a notorious human trafficker, pedophile, and hedge fund billionaire who dies in a prison cell. In fact, I find Jeffrey

Epstein perfectly affable—perhaps only odd in his choice of friends, who include a hulking, muscular menace as wide as he is tall. Bristling with muscle and possessing no visible neck, he is often waiting for Jeffrey outside the school gates. When I ask Jeffrey about him, he just smiles.

We call him Neutral because his mind is not in gear.

———·———

Darkness of a much more personal kind is around the corner for me. In my sophomore year at Dalton, busily not living up to my potential, I win a field opportunity award in zoology, given by the world-famous Explorer's Club. The win affords me the opportunity to join one of a number of scientific expeditions funded by the club. I choose a zoological survey of the Chaco Boreal region of Paraguay, a vast, thorny jungle the Encyclopedia Britannica likens to hell on Earth. Prior to the trip, my parents take me to meet the expedition leader. RWM is a mammologist at the University of Connecticut and a senior biologist at the Smithsonian Institution. These two establishments, along with the Explorer's Club and *National Geographic* magazine, support RMW's field research. I discover RMW, a gentile who has devoted himself to the study of tropical mammals, has an upright piano covered with dust and a wife who serves teabags who seems much nicer than he is. I don't like the smell of his house and I don't like the smell of his clothes.

RMW tells my parents about where I will be going.

The Chaco is a rough place. Beautiful, but challenging in any season. There are many deadly snakes, jaguars, and, of course, vampire bats.

My mother goes slightly pale. RMW does nothing to reassure her, a fact I will reflect upon later as a missed signal that there was something wrong with the man and something wrong with the opportunity, too. By the time I discover all that, it will be too late.

Oh yes. Of course, they're not giants like in the movies. They don't block moonbeams with their wings or anything. They're actually mouse-sized creatures with razor-sharp teeth that alight on our exposed flesh while we sleep. Their saliva contains a numbing agent, like a mosquito's, but so much stronger we don't feel the bite. That's the problem, of course, because many of them are rabid.

At this point, my father interrupts.

Rabies is a fatal disease.

RMW nods.

Exactly so, which is why the boy will need to be vaccinated before he joins us.

My father arranges for me to receive a rabies vaccine at New York Hospital. When the time comes, I'm presented with six syringes neatly laid out in a row on a kidney-shaped metal dish, and I'm told they go in my stomach.

I don't want them in the stomach.

My father is grimly insistent.

If you really want to go to that godforsaken place, then you need the vaccine. No vaccine, no expedition. There's nothing else to say.

In the end, I accept the shots only if they give them to me in the arm. Three on each side. They hurt going in, but at first, I think they will be ok. During the car ride home, they throb. During the night, my arms swell crazily. They hurt so much even a brush of air sets them on fire. My mother hears me whimpering and comes in to take my temperature. Seeing it so high, she wakes my father. He visits if I'm thirsty. When I down half a liter of water, he just nods.

This is what you wanted, so don't complain. Real rabies feels like this only a hundred times worse. It gets nastier and nastier until you die in agony.

The agony of the vaccine is a harbinger of worse to come. In fact, Paraguay spells trouble for me before I even get to the remote jungle research station that will serve as our basecamp. At an apartment in the capital city of Asunción, we organize what we need for the work, making preparations for permits and transportation and the like. The expeditioners are openly resentful about having me tied to their research grant from the Explorer's Club—a real albatross around their necks. Worse, they don't like kids from well-off families, and they especially don't like Jews.

We leave the city at dawn by truck. Morning to night we jolt our way across the Trans-Chaco Highway, a red dirt road deeply rutted down the middle and even with tires the size of a Great Dane, we are in constant danger of being high-centered. It's June, winter in the Southern Hemisphere. The road is dry as a bone and throws up clouds of red dust. Hundreds of miles go by like this. The scientists drink endless bottles of beer. I'm given a single soda the whole day and no water; I'm dry as a crisp by lunchtime. By starlight, a stiff wind would blow me away like a fallen autumn leaf.

At dusk we arrive at camp—two buildings and a lean-to. The buildings are roughly made of wooden boards that offers no protection from the wind. The roof fits like an adult's ball cap on a twelve-year-old. One building is mostly for storage, the other has bunks. Both have dirt floors. After I help offload supplies from the truck, I'm pointed at the lean-to and told I don't get to sleep inside. Still buzzing from their day-long guzzle, the guys decide they want to keep on buzzing and set off to the local Mennonite colony, Filadelfia, for more beer.

Just like that, I'm in the middle of the Chaco Boreal of Paraguay, alone under a night sky that shows me stars from horizon to horizon, shaming the planetarium at the American Museum of Natural History back in New York, and leaving me completely terrified. The temperature is dropping fast, so I gather fallen branches from a dense green tree called Palo Santo, whose fragrance is what God uses for aromatherapy. I use a plastic cigarette lighter to get the fire going in a pit. The smoke is thick and distorts the stars into a swarming acid trip of celestial lights. The fire girds me against the cold and the stars make me think of Master Po.

I'm speaking out loud to Po when wolves appear. I figure the camping supplies must be drawing them, in particular the scientists' seemingly endless boxes of beef jerky. They are South American maned wolves, and they prey primarily on smaller mammals. I know this because the purpose of our expedition is to survey everything that is living in this thorny jungle, and I've done my homework. At fifty pounds each, they are small for wolves, more like really big foxes. Still, in the dark, in a pack with eyes glowing, long legs, huge ears and lower canines the size of toothbrushes, their howling and growling is the stuff of nightmares for a young Manhattanite who has never even been camping. I keep them at bay by lighting sticks on fire, but what finally got the wolves to back off was not so much the fire but the dawn. Like movie vampires, along with the bloodsuckers flitting around, the first light of day has them melting into the surrounding brush.

My crew comes back midmorning. I hope they have breakfast for me but all they do is point unceremoniously at a box of wheat cereal while they nurse hangovers and drink enough coffee to float a Staten Island ferryboat. At last, RMW sets me to running trap lines. This means hiding twenty to thirty snap traps to catch small animals. I have never set a snap trap. I use peanut butter for the trap tab and my hands get a bit slippery from the oil. Inevitably, I lose traction on a spring bar, and the thing slips out and closes on my finger, bruising it badly. This is how a mouse must feel right at the end: useless. I wonder, fleetingly, if simply existing means fulfilling a purpose in the universe or, as I've been told, life is really all about money and celebrity and power. I also feel lousy for mice.

Trapping is my job for weeks on end. It would be a straightforward business, despite the challenge of trying to remember where I have put the traps, if the rest of the crew were not clandestinely plotting ways to torture me for the sins of class privilege and winning the Explorer's Club award. After the first week, WL tells me something new in his slow Georgia drawl.

> There really is not enough food for you to have breakfast like the rest of us. We have to save the milk and cereal. After all, we got a baby now.

It's true that there is a baby, as PH's wife has joined the group along with her infant. She knows there's plenty of food, though, and won't look me in the eye. She seems particularly uncomfortable while cooking at daybreak while I am banished to the perimeter of camp like an ill-mannered dog. I steal some little snacks during the day but it's not easy with the new mother always eyeing the granary. A week goes by, and RM has some news for me, which is accompanied by a gesture toward the thorn jungle all around us.

> Go on and find your own food. You're not having any more of ours. Also, I don't want you sleeping too much, so go ahead and take overnight temperature readings every four hours right on through the night.

> But it goes up to a hundred and down to freezing at night.

> I'll need you to document that precisely all day and night.

The next morning, I wake writhing with stomach cramps and covered in dust. There has been a big windstorm during the night. The rest of the men have not endured it as they are all safely inside with the woman and baby, while I'm under the open lean-to and totally exposed. There is a rifle at camp, a .22lr with a .410 shotgun barrel. I know how to shoot reasonably well, though all I have ever used is an air rifle, so I go out looking for something to eat. Right at this moment, I'm not thinking about how I'm going to clean and cook whatever it may be; I'm just ravenous and need to eat. I spend the day running my trap lines. I find some dead mice and voles in my traps, but I'm not yet hungry enough to force myself to eat them. I write collection data on each animal and bag it. Late afternoon, I come across a baby armadillo so cute I can't kill it. I bring it back to camp and let it loose in the main building where the makeshift kitchen is. The guys like it and fuss over what food they can give it. They watch it eat with evident delight. It grunts contentedly while eating the food they give it. They make a little bed for it out of a blanket in the corner; it curls up and goes to sleep.

I go out again at dusk. I see a big multicolored locust on a branch. I have been told these insects swarm in biblical numbers and wonder whether I will see a huge cloud of them. I grab it. It looks way too hard to chew. My stomach growls. The sky darkens. Frogs call. I follow the sound to a marshy area and find a little toad sitting on top of a cow pie. Grabbing it, I end up with the toad, but also with shit all over my hand. I secure the toad in a cloth bag and tuck the bag in my belt. Toads are toxic, so not a food item. I want to show the toad to RMW. I want to prove my worth and please him. Perhaps this is about my father, perhaps it's something else. Either way, I feel like a supplicant and it's humiliating.

Rinsing my hand in the marshy water, I hear a low growl. There is only one animal in this jungle that makes a sound like that. The rifle is resting beside me on the driest patch of grass I could find. I lift it slowly, knowing that with its small caliber it might not do more than piss off a jaguar. I turn around slowly. I look around in the dim light. I see a reticulated flash, white and brown, and then nothing. I head back down the path to camp. Half an hour later, in the little light that is left, a see a tamandua in my path. The beautiful anteater is as surprised to see me as I am to see it. Perhaps it discerns that I'm not one of the indigenous Guarani people that have been part of the Paraguayan landscape for thousands of years.

A Guarani Indian is part of our team. Mitiki serves as a local guide. Self-sufficient in the extreme, living on his horse like a latter-day New World Mongol, he wears his woolen poncho by day and sleeps in it by night, his head on a rolled-up pack dangling from his belt. He has a rifle, too, but it's a more serious piece of business than the one that I have, and he no doubt shoots a lot better than I do. A kinship has formed between me and Mitiki. His English is pretty much nonexistent, and his Spanish is often too heavily accented for me to understand, but he seems to sense my situation. I ponder this daily, our lives so completely opposite—he could not imagine the comforts and luxuries I'm accustomed nor I his poverty. At the same time, I sense no ill will in him, no envy. He seems to know he is freer than I will ever be.

The tamandua qualifies as a large mammal, one I know will be of great interest to RMW, but I don't raise my rifle right away. It regards me with evident consciousness; it appears intelligent, awake, and alert. I don't want to shoot it. I take a long draught of water that I carry in a screw-top jar in my backpack, hoping that perhaps the movement will scare it off. This is not the clean water from camp—I'm not allowed to drink that—but the murky liquid from a nearby pond. There are so many bugs in it, I have to strain them with my teeth. I exhale loudly, but even that does not drive the tamandua away. I raise the rifle. I concentrate on the front sight, which is what you are supposed to do when aiming, rather than looking at the live animal being fifty feet away. I squeeze the trigger. Shotgun pellets fly. They strike the animal in the chest and head. It drops to its side and its legs kick spasmodically. I feel like I want to vomit. I sit down on the ground at a distance and wait for it to stop moving. When it does, I pick it up by the tail and bring it back to camp. I toss it at RMW's feet like a pet cat bringing its owner a canary. I deeply regret both killing it and seeking the approval of a man of such low character.

The scientists continue to treat me this way. I find something to eat here and there: a grapefruit, a biscuit, some small fish I catch in the pond and cook on the fire.

After a couple of weeks of this, I catch a cold. Because I am asthmatic, the cold goes to my lungs and conditions have reduced my immune system, and I spike a fever. I cough up thick green mucus. It's hard to breathe as I'm wheezing so badly. I freeze at night and roast during the day, and nobody does a thing to help me. PH's wife actually tells the men to keep me away from the building where the food is because she does not want me coughing on the infant. I come to realize that this is not a nightmare; it's real. If I die here, which is what they all seem to want, they can simply say I had a fatal asthma attack or wandered off into the bush one morning, never to be seen again. I can't believe these are senior scientists working for august institutions and that they are actually going through with this *Lord of the Flies*-type action. I grow sicker and weaker.

A few days later, I hear the Cessna that comes out our way every week to drop a burlap sack of mail for the group. The letters I have received from this pilot have mostly been from my Grandpa Arthur, the famous cardiologist after whom I am named and who is now dying horribly of pancreatic cancer. Each time I get something from him, his writing becomes more and more like chicken scratch—harder and harder to read, lighter in the imprint, the individual characters larger and more poorly defined. He avoids complaining or speculating about his prognosis, but he does mention that he now weighs only eighty pounds and takes quite a bit of morphine. Hearing the plane, I leave the camp, follow the sound, and go to the open area where the pilot drops the bag. I wave at him desperately. He circles. I wave some more. He lands.

I have only a few minutes to run back and collect my stuff. There is a tense moment during which I'm not sure the scientists are going to let me go. I can see on their faces that they are thinking through the consequences of my escape. What will I say? Will I reveal what has happened here? If I do, who will believe me? A teenager's word against those of well-regarded research academicians? He was delusional, they will say. Feverish. He suffers from a personality disorder. He's a pampered kid from Park Avenue. He wasn't expecting the Chaco to be so rough, was neither emotionally nor physically prepared for its rigors. It was all we could to keep the baby safe from him. He tried to sabotage our work.

I have run this scenario through my head dozens of times. I leave most of my stuff behind, taking only my Puma hunting knife, my money, passport, and clothes for a couple of days. RMW follows me to the airplane, but once the pilot has landed and can see what is going on, makes no effort to stop me climbing aboard. The plane is set up for light cargo and mail. There is no seat for me. The pilot, shocked by my appearance, gestures for me to lie down in the back between the remaining canvas mail sacks. As the engine starts up, I can hear RMW's last words to me.

You're one tough little son of a bitch.

My fever is so high, I remember very little of the flight, but know that a few hours later, I'm delivered to the embassy with a high fever. The embassy doctor is called, and I'm admitted to a private Catholic hospital. The doctor is Nicolas Breuer, a Paraguayan aristocrat of German descent. He saves my life by treating my pneumonia and fever with antibiotics and intravenous steroids. When I leave the hospital, he tells me to fly home. I tell him my ticket back is not for another few weeks, and that I want to go back out to the Chaco.

THE MONK OF PARK AVENUE

What I don't tell him is what those bastards did to me. I don't tell him that I want to show them they can't beat me. He says I'm crazy, says I will relapse and die if I go back out there to the harsh temperatures, the dust, the wind. He invites me to stay at his home, a warm and rambling place with walls of pale green, native woods in abundance, woven wool blankets in multiple colors, and a kitchen like Grand Central Station. When he finds out who my father and grandfather are, he calls New York and gives them an update. He has nine children. One of them, his oldest son who is also named Nicolas, is the only one missing. I sleep in his bed, but I enjoy spending time with all the rest of the Breuer kids, flaring my poncho like a cape and pretending to be the vampire Barnabas Collins from the daytime TV drama *Dark Shadows*, popular down there at the time. I'm made to feel part of the family. The doctor's wife mothers me. Beatrice is a fantastic woman and calls me "number ten."

All my childhood vignettes are subsumed within the much larger narrative of my father's evolving career, which is, in turn, grounded within the narrative of the lives of his own Holocaust-survivor parents—simultaneously tragic and heroic figures. My grandmother, Vera, born to a family of accomplished Viennese intellectuals, loses her identical twin and the rest of her family to the Holocaust. She meets my Russian grandfather, and they have tough times in Russia, Austria, and Poland before finally emigrating to Canada because the US will take no more Jews. She makes a living renting a room in her house in Montreal. As long as I know her, every time she laughs, she finishes with a sigh. Survivor's guilt is, for her, utterly unquenchable. It will dog her as long as she lives.

Vera is sometimes judgmental and sharp-tongued but is an unfailingly adoring grandmother, generous of time and energy. She is also desperately proud of my father, whose burgeoning success is a salve for her pain, something that apparently makes her feel as if all she's been through was worth it in some way. One evening, while I am still in high school, my father invites her to dinner with some international bigwigs and I tag along. Present are the Soviet Ambassador to the United Nations, the Soviet Ambassador to the United States, and the Soviet Minister of Health. It is an impressive crowd but given her history, Vera is no great fan of Russians. I sit next to her, across the table from the dignitaries. She doesn't like the food and keeps spitting pieces of chicken into her napkin and surreptitiously tossing them under the table. I notice this and glance down to see the spit-out chicken landing on the polished shoes of the ambassador. I ask her how she likes the food. She hisses at me.

Shut up.

Her husband, Moishe, is a five-foot-two pushcart-peddler-turned-farm equipment-vendor selling his wares out of a warehouse in rural Ontario. His past, however, is dramatic and checkered. The son of a shylock, he and his brother spend their teens smuggling diamonds and gold across the border between Russia and Poland. The band of boys gathered around them are affectionately called Moishe's Militia. Returning from a smuggling foray one day, they find their village in ruins. The Russian Tsar's private army, Tatar soldiers called Cossacks, has come to the village and engaged in a so-called *pogrom* against the hated

Jews: raping women, burning houses, and murdering men. In a rage, my grandfather and his gang use their intimate knowledge of the forest to track and ambush these fierce fighters, shooting them from arboreal hides and erasing the troop, becoming hunted outlaws as a result.

In a later chapter of Moishe's life, he shoots Russian soldiers in the back as they flee from him on the railroad tracks after trying to rape my grandmother and her sister. He is a meek and mild-mannered man, and I can never believe he was an equestrian tough guy, a leader of a militia that protected Jews. Never, that is, until I bring home a mouse to feed my pet monitor lizard, a three-foot predator with a roving, tasting tongue, fierce jaws, and sharp teeth. Moishe is visiting and I invite him to watch. I put the mouse on the floor of my bedroom while I get the lizard out of his tank. The encounter is dramatic. The reptile moves sinuously across the light carpet. The mouse sniffs the world, hopefully clueless that she is about to die. The lizard grows closer. His tongue flicks in and out. Suddenly, Grandpa Moishe is off the bed like a rocket, fists pumping in the air, screaming, his eyes bugged wide.

Chase him! Bite him! Kill him!

I have the distinct impression that all Jews, no matter what material gains they have made in the world or the esteem in which they are held in their community, subconsciously fear the early-morning pounding on the door that will take it all away. Seeing the assassin hiding in my little grandfather's rumpled clothing, I see where I get my taste for the martial, the steel wrapped in cotton I will increasingly have, the deeper I descend into the world I have chosen. I recognize I'm not content with the role of the fearful Jew, the multi-

SPONGE IN A HURRICANE

generational legacy of Hitler's Holocaust. I know my father isn't, as social status is a (perhaps illusory) form of security, and my father continues to crave it more with each passing year. I see him as a tree whose roots are his family but whose trunk is his professional and political power, and whose branches are his patients and whose leaves are his friends. Adulation is the water that makes everything grow, and the more celebrity he attains, the more of that water there is.

Toward the end of my time in high school, my father's efforts pay off. His path to the Big Time seems serendipitous, but if so, it is only the way that success eventually comes to anyone who repeatedly positions him or herself in its path. The door to that path is one Antenor Patiño, a Bolivian business magnate who inherits an empire from his father, the so-called King of Tin. Through revolution, rebellion, and more, Patiño builds his fortune and uses it to fraternize with the European jet set and build Mexican resorts. Trouble is, he can't keep up with any of this—he is slipping due to a heart condition.

The way my father relates it, Patiño's regular doctor has the rich man's problem all wrong. Seeing the mistake, my father orders the nurse to change the treatment. The nurse balks, as Patiño's physician is a more senior man. Overhearing the exchange, Patiño tells the nurse to do what my father says. When he makes a full and rapid recovery, Patiño spreads the word about the young Jewish doctor to his elite cohort. Pretty soon, the international jet streams to my father's consulting office in droves.

They're not the only ones, of course. Not to be outdone by counts and countesses, dukes and duchesses, princes and princesses, and a myriad of other continental celebrities, America's own elite gradually fill my father's medical practice

THE MONK OF PARK AVENUE

as well. Politicians show up at our third Manhattan apartment at 510 Park Avenue, along with a bevy of business moguls, kings, princes, ministers, Hollywood stars, ambassadors, and dignitaries. My father prevails upon his well-heeled patients to make generous donations to New York Hospital and Cornell's medical school. Through these efforts he becomes a force to be reckoned in those hallowed halls, where he teaches future doctors about the importance of compassion—a quality in increasingly short supply—and the critical role of the physical exam, a fading practice.

The summer after the one I spent in the Chaco, I work as a file clerk in my father's office. The job entails pulling manila files from the big, tan, steel cabinets in advance of appointments and returning them to the cabinets at day's end. The files contain lab results, my father's diagnoses and treatment records, contact information, and billing statements. On my first day, I notice that perhaps a third of the files have an orange sticker on them: the sort of paper disk you might see bearing price at a garage sale. I ask one of the office workers what the sticker means and she refers me to the office manager. The manager tells me to ask my father, so I knock on the door of his consulting office in order to do so.

> May I ask you about those orange stickers on the patient files?

> Can't you see I'm busy with a patient?

I ask a few more times but everyone stonewalls me. Finally, the young guy who runs my father's office laboratory takes pity on me.

> Those stickers are for patients like old Sadie from Brooklyn who was in today. They don't have any money to pay, so your father doesn't charge them.

But he has so many rich patients. Are you saying he steals from the rich?

He doesn't steal from anyone. He gives everyone great care. He just looks after the poor out of his own pocket.

Some of the wealthy celebrities who fund my father's largess are fixtures in my life even before high school. Our family is often in the company of the actor Danny Kaye and his brilliant wife, Sylvia, who teaches me much about plotting and screenwriting in my early years as a writer. Danny likes to tell people that my father is completely out of touch with popular culture, something I inherit from him. One time, I'm at the Kayes' home in Beverly Hills having dinner with my father, Danny, and the comedian George Burns. The doorbell rings and my father gets up to answer it. He returns to report that there's a scruffy-looking guy with long hair and wearing blue jeans at the door. Danny narrows his eyes.

What's his name?

John Denver.

Danny goes crazy.

That guy has sold more records than anyone in the history of the world and you leave him standing outside?? Never answer the door at my house again!

A few more guests arrive, and my father stays away from the door. The singer Vikki Carr is there, along with Mick Jagger. My father asks Mick Jagger what he does for a living.

I'm a musician.

Really? How's that going for you?

Pretty well, actually...

During my last few months of high school, the Greek shipping tycoon Aristotle Onassis appears at our door. I lead him to my father, who tapes his eyelids up as treatment for myasthenia gravis, a muscle-wasting disease. Afterward, he wants more of my father's company.

Jackie is in the limo downstairs. Let's go somewhere for dinner.

My father calls David Keh, a Chinese restaurateur he has known since he was a waiter at Four Seas, a Cantonese place down on Maiden Lane in the financial district. Keh has a bodyguard and carries a gun, having successfully fended off Tong gangs to establish a group of top-flight Chinese places in Manhattan. These include *Uncle Tai's Hunan Yuan*, his Third Avenue flagship, and *Pig Heaven*, a dumpling house in midtown. My father reserves a table at the latter but exacts a promise from Keh that he will not call the paparazzi. When my mother declines to go, my father invites me along. We sneak into the place and have a meal. Afterward, I leave with Jackie O, the widow of President JFK, on my arm. Despite his promise, Keh couldn't help himself and paparazzi are waiting. Flashes go off in my face. I shield myself. Jacqueline Kennedy Onassis sails through the chaos like Queen Mary on a still pond. The caption in a New York newspaper the next morning reads: "Jackie O in Chinese Orgy with Bearded Hippie."

During those same few months, I'm at my father's office one day when Zero Mostel, star of the stage and screen, bursts through the outside door like a triple-wide trailer chased by a twister. He surveys the waiting room, which is full of people on couches and chairs reading magazines or talking quietly. He approaches the desk and announces he is here for his appointment. The receptionist asks his name. He replies with an indignant look.

Zero Mostel.

She gestures toward an empty chair, implying he should wait like everyone else. He nods, smiles then asks a favor.

Do you happen to have a flashlight?

A flashlight?

Precisely.

She leaves the desk and returns with an Eveready torch, the kind with a metal tube and a red plastic head. Mostel takes it, positions himself in the center of the waiting room, and begins to remove his clothes. Standing, obese, in only his undershorts, he plunges the flashlight down next to his manhood and turns it on. His nether regions glow red, and he begins screaming.

It burns, oy how it burns!

He is immediately ushered into my father's consulting room. Patiently waiting along with everyone else is not for him.

My high school girlfriend, Diane, also knows Zero. I meet her a few weeks after returning from Paraguay. We start dating, and one afternoon she calls to excitedly tell me that Bob Dylan and The Band are coming to Madison Square Garden. I reach the venue ten minutes after the tickets go on sale and find the show sold out. Back home, I ask my father if he knows anyone at the Garden. He is working at his desk at home and doesn't even look up.

Write down what it is, when it is, who it is.

I give him the information, and pretty much forget about it. A few months later, on the night of the concert, I head out to take Diane to dinner. My father is once again in his home office and has a clear view of the foyer. He sees me pass.

Where are you off to?

I have a date.

Where do you think you're going?

I have a dinner date with Diane.

Sit down.

Dad. I have a date and I'm going to be late.

I have a date. Come in here and sit down, he says.

Just sit for a bit.

Ostentatiously, I check my wristwatch and tap my foot. He doesn't look up from whatever he's doing. I make a move to the bench by the elevator. He can still see me. I haven't left the apartment. A few minutes go by. I stand up. This time, he yells.

Sit down and wait!

This behavior is highly unusual. My father pretty much never knows where I'm going or when, and never seems to care. I chafe. I have dinner reservations at the Magic Pan, a crêperie on Third Avenue and I'm excited about it. I'm about to stand up again when the elevator door opens. A long-haired man wearing jeans, a white oxford, a blue blazer, and penny loafers steps out.

Are you Arthur?

Speechless, the best I can do is nod.

Well, Bobby gave me these tickets, but I've got other plans.

Paul McCartney hands me a pair of tickets and is back in the elevator before I can manage any more than a weak thank you. This may be the most dramatic one, but there are so many other great opportunities to enjoy the people in my father's orbit. To a seeker like me, it is all grist for the mill, a smorgasbord courtesy of my father's career and one I could scarcely imagine finding on my own. Alexander Lieberman, creative director of the Conde Nast empire, is a fixture and a writing mentor to me during high school and beyond, and his marvelous giant metal sculptures adorn our apartment and our country home in Westchester County. Lieberman talks to me quite a bit about writing and about art, while diplomat extraordinaire Richard Holbrooke is another family friend from whom I learn about the world—not art and writing, but the global balance of power. Philosopher and psychologist Erich Fromm explains to me the difference between morality and obedience with authority, a theme I take into my novels and nonfiction books. The writer Jerzy Kosinski visits from time to time, as does another Nobel laureate, exiled Russian poet Joseph Brodsky. The actor Walter Matthau drops by frequently. He looks so much like my father that the two of them are frequently mistaken for each other in public and take perverse pleasure in signing the other's name when an autograph is requested. The immortal Sophia Loren is another screen star who comes by from time to time, and the sculptor Jacques Lipschitz gives my parents some beautiful pieces. The "King of Italy" Gianni Agnelli—he owns FIAT, Ferrari, and newspapers—regularly appears at our home with his wife, as does Count Teo Rossi, principle in the liquor brand Martini & Rossi, an ebullient and charming man.

During my final high school spring break, my family cruises the Mediterranean on Rossi's yacht, *Tritona*, a converted minesweeper. A Rembrandt hangs in the salon and there is a wide, white leather couch at her stern. One afternoon, we anchor off the coast of the Greek island Mykonos. Beautiful people parade on the beach against a backdrop of whitewashed buildings. The declining sun does what no alchemist in history has ever been able to do; it turns the Mediterranean to gold. Rich kids play on jet skis nearby. Rossi assumes the central position on the white couch, sitting where the ship's wheel would be if this were an eighteenth-century frigate.

His family and our family join him. There is plenty of room for all. White-gloved waiters materialize like ghosts from the salon, bearing silver trays. The count introduces us to his feast in his lilting, Italian-accented English.

I had this smoke salmon flown in from Scotland by helicopter for you. These olives and tomatoes and this feta cheese are fresh from the island.

A moment later, a wine steward appears: a cloth over his arm, bottle in hand, and a bucket of ice, too. He uncorks a bottle of Château d'Yquem, a libation produced by the same family at the same vineyard for more than four centuries. My father, who fancies himself a connoisseur of the divine nectar, nearly jumps out of his skin. Recently, he has joined the *Confrérie des Chevaliers du Tastevin*, a rowdy bunch of Burgundy fans. The count sniffs the cork and nods. The steward pours a sip for the count to approve, which he does. The count plunges his old hand into the ice bucket and sprinkles cubes and chips into his glass. My father jumps off the couch, unable to contain himself.

Not ice! Not in the Château d'Yquem!

The count is undeterred. Holding his glass aloft, he sets my father straight.

Dottore. Sometimes you know something, and sometimes you just think you know something. These Sauternes are very high in sugar. When you put in ice, the wine fractionates. The bottom, clear layer is the water. The yellow layer on top of that is the wine. The top layer of sugar, this thin brown meniscus? This is what God has for dessert.

He takes a demitasse spoon, scoops that top layer, and shoves it into my father's mouth. My father's eyes fly open.

That's the most delicious thing I've ever tasted.

He says as a frisson of pleasure shakes him. Count Rossi puts down the spoon, leans back, and spreads his arms over the couch. He surveys his yacht, his staff, his family. He gazes at the golden sea before him and the beautiful sights in every direction. He takes a deep breath and lets out a long sigh.

Born to suffer.

Applied to our family's privileges, the phrase becomes a humorous, self-deprecating meme in my family. It doesn't sit so well with me. Although I can laugh about the absurdity of the wealth I'm exposed to, there is an abiding unease in me. I know we live an exceptional life and travel the world on vacations, but the Guarani Indian Mitiki hovers at the back of mind, as does Master Po and, of course, the horrors of the Holocaust, where my forbears are not only stripped bare of their possessions but of their lives. I can't find balance in any of this—not the gap between rich and poor nor the attachment to objects and opportunities of favor.

I long to harmonize the feelings of safety and stability I enjoy in contrast to that of many others in the world but find it no mean task that I'm becoming increasingly uncomfortable with the gap between rich and poor and with the attachment to objects of favor. I see my Unk in near despair after his late mother's collection of Ming dynasty snuff bottles is stolen from his Manhattan storage unit, and I see my father's pride in his nice clothes and shoes. I see my own tendencies to follow suit, my urge to collect things, my impatience and impulsiveness and grasping, and it generates self-loathing of a particular sort. I see it as a weakness in myself, one which Master Po would never tolerate. Even more, it just doesn't seem that such trappings bring happiness, even though I am told they do.

This lesson comes to a head when, in the summer before college, I meet Elizinha Gonçalves Salles. She is the glamorous wife of Brazilian banker, politician, and philanthropist Walter Moreira Salles, a formative contributor to the development of Brazil's financial powerhouse. No teenage boy, indeed, no master of the universe, could possibly fail to be entranced by her. Elizinha brings me a book on King Louis XIV, the so-called Sun King, and speaks to me about the importance of being surrounded by beautiful things.

I pay a social visit to the Salles family at their compound outside of Rio de Janeiro. It is a far gentler South American adventure than my time in Paraguay. I'm treated with love and care, and I get to see a little bit of the town, too. Walter Jr., Elizinha's son, shows me how a Brazilian society teen lives by taking me for a death-defying sports car ride, scattering farm animals and field workers with entitled glee. Walter Jr.

goes on to become a film director who romanticizes the youth of Argentine revolutionary and homophobe Che Guevara. Elizinha later takes her own life. Long before Elizinha dies, however, I begin to doubt that fame and fortune lead to happiness. I wonder how much of the unhappiness I see is the result of a disconnect from nature, but I can't say that in these early days I can frame it that clearly. I just notice that having it all is surely better than having nothing, but even so, the rich and famous are often depressed, fractious, lonely, and insubstantial at the core.

The failings and flaws I notice in others are never nearly as painful as the ones I notice in myself. I seem unable to enact the changes I know I must in order to become the person I want to be. I'm constantly falling into the same traps I see in the people around me: pride of ownership, obsession with nice things, obsessive control over my own micro-environment, such as it exists while still living under my parents' wing and in their home. The time I spend coveting things, the time I spend worrying over trivial external issues disappoints me. I think about the simplicity of Mitiki's life and his knowledge of all that is real in the trees and the jaguars, the herbs, the anteaters, and the fish. I know that being surrounded by the stuff of man, the concocted agendas, the pressures on a young man about to step out into the world and prove himself—first in academia and then in commerce— seem false and shallow. They seem to me, spoiled by my fortunate circumstances as I may be, to be the wrong path.

I've been fortunate in my applications to college and have a choice of Ivy League schools. Perhaps one of them will lead to me living up to my potential! At length I choose Yale for the excellence of its writing programs as well as the zoology and anthropology departments. All of these fit my diffuse but connected interests. During that blurry time when I am no longer a boy but also not yet a man, that last summer in New York City, I have one last reminder that life can contain layers right where I stand, that I don't have to travel to find spirituality, truth, shamanism, gritty power or look to a television character to find them. This reminder involves one Maria Carlos de Jesus, my parents' longtime, live-in housekeeper. Maria is a diminutive Colombian woman of Indian descent, a devout Catholic and self-proclaimed virgin who nightly retreats to a bedroom cluttered with crosses. I hear whispers about Maria from other people who float in and out of our lives, helping my mother to run the home of a luminous physician and take care of four children. They center around the notion that Maria's uncompromising moral strictness and chastity has somehow given her authority over the Colombian community of the 1960s and '70s.

Finally, mere weeks before I matriculate to Yale, the bell rings at the service entrance to the apartment. I open the door to find a couple of leather-jacketed street toughs standing with their hands in their pockets, looking sheepish. They ask for Maria, so I go and get her. When they see all four-foot-ten of her, standing in a white housemaid's dress, they start to tremble. She points a finger at them, and their knees actually buckle. I understand enough Spanish to glean that these are Colombian drug runners. *Narcotraficantes*. Bad dudes, probably packing guns and knives.

Maria points to the sky and addresses them in a strong voice.

> The Father and the Son and the Heavenly Ghost are watching you. They know what you think about all day, they know about your lusts and your crimes and transgressions. They know all the evil that you do. If you

want to be forgiven, if you want not to roast in Hell for all eternity, you must change your ways right now. You must get honest jobs. You must start sending money back to your families in Colombia.

When she's finished rendering her judgment, the tough guys, chastened and groveling, are afraid even to wait for the elevator. Instead, they go back down the stairs. When they are out of sight (their footsteps say there are running, taking the steps two or three at a time), once we can hear no more of them, Maria closes the door, locks it, and turns to me.

And you. You must leave this home now and be a man. You must stop asking questions and start finding answers. You must figure out your own way to Heaven. You cannot go in circles forever. You have to find your way.

She might as well be Master Po.

CHAPTER 2

A PANOPLY OF
POSSIBILITIES

E very other year, TC, a a famous, career-making editor
who works at a big New York house and at a popular
magazine, offers a fiction-writing workshop to Yale
students in their third year. If you are a junior during one of
TC's off years, there's nothing for it. If, on the other hand, you
are there when he is there, and your writing sample garners
you one of the ten spots in the workshop, luck is your middle
name. Problem is, out of the 1,200 people in my class, two
thirds of them are English majors—Yale is humanities-centric
after all—and many of them are damn fine writers, at least for
college students. With so much competition, it is kill-or-be-
killed in the mad struggle to be selected for his class.

I am given a spot, no doubt because TC wants a certain
mix and I fit his bill. It proves to be an instructive workshop,
perhaps the most useful I take at Yale. Pompous and self-
congratulatory, TC is nonetheless a marvelous teacher and a
great editor. He cuts right to the chase, pulls no punches, and

spares no inspiration. You can obviously write, he inscribes in red pen on one of my stories, but do you really have anything to say? He asks this because he has already announced, and apparently believes, that by the time a writer is five years old, he or she already knows all they will ever need to know to be a great short-story author or novelist. Everything I learn in my years after Yale tells me that this is utter and complete nonsense, but now, with stars in my eyes, I and all the other students believe it.

A couple of years later, when I have graduated and am working as a science teacher at Dalton (my first alma mater) I decide to pursue a Master of Fine Arts at the Columbia University Writing Program. After I complete my application, I go see TC at his office and ask if he will put in a good word for me. He tells me he will do so with pleasure. A week later, I get a letter from him in the mail. It tells me that I should give up the idea of being a writer and find something else to do with my life. He says that a whole other constellation of impulses will soon seize me, and I will forget all about the literary life.

I'm devastated by this epistle and wonder whether TC is just placing an obstacle in my path so as to help me summon the kind of dedication, sacrifice, and resolve it takes to be a true writer. In his megalomania, TC really does see himself as a kingmaker; he may really believe this kind of manipulation is not only his job but also his mission. I also wonder whether he senses in me something I sense in myself but try to suppress. Does he know about the presence of Master Po in the back of my head, constantly steering my ship in classic what-would-Jesus-do fashion, or does he detect in me how much the narcissism so rampant in the New York literary scene of the 1980s really turns me off? I don't exactly fit the bill for club membership, sporting as I do an utterly different sensibility. I have become aware of so much that needs fixing in the world, so much that needs help and attention and effort—whether it be human suffering or the persecution of the natural world. I can't help but feel that the desire to see one's words in print, be adulated for them in *The New York Times*, and be celebrated at cocktail parties is not exactly the path for me.

TC's letter made it all the more shocking and unpalatable when I get a call from a Yale classmate who happens to work in the dean's office of the very program at Columbia that interests me.

I don't know exactly how to tell you this.

My friend says,

But today my boss got a call from TC saying that under absolutely no circumstances should you be admitted to the program. I'm not, in fact, admitted, and I take it to be a blessing. Perhaps TC's instincts are right and his intentions good, even if his methods leave something to be desired.

A few years after this episode, Simon & Schuster publishes my first book. Unk throws me a book party at his Sutton Place apartment. I invite a bunch of family and friends, my editor, and TC. Unk has the event catered, at least libations and canapes, and a beautiful blonde works the bar. I'm about to get something from her when TC magically appears ahead of me in line and asks her a question.

Didn't I sleep with you at the Iowa Writer's Conference?

To her undying credit—and to my everlasting regret that I never got her name and asked her out—she looks him up and down, pauses the scan halfway, and answers without skipping a beat.

Not that I would remember.

———·———

One particular weekend, I come down from Yale to visit my Great Uncle Frank at Overbrook Farm, his Connecticut home. Overbrook is a magnificent property; eight hundred acres of prime real estate that later becomes an Audubon preserve and will always hold a special place in my heart. When I'm nine years old, it is the experience of canoeing on the river and running through the beautiful property early that yields my first interaction with a painted turtle, the reptile that starts me on the path to Daoist nature worship. In addition to a boathouse on the river, there is a printing press for fine works of intellection, a fire station devoted solely to the property, and a gymnasium with a small bowling alley. Waiting for lunch to be served, I wander into the gym. It has not been used in years and there is a thick layer of dust everywhere. I notice a small door to the right of the bowling pins. I figure it gives lane access to set up the pins, but it seems in the wrong size for that, being hobbit-sized, rounded at the top, painted green, and made of vertical slats like an old barndoor for a miniature horse. The padlock hanging off its hasp comes free when I tug it.

I bend over and pass through.

The wash of light from the gym reveals a spiral staircase going down. There is a string hanging from the ceiling and I tug it. A bare bulb lights the way down. I had not imagined there would be a basement under the bowling alley, but here it is. I find another string hanging at the bottom of the staircase, and when I tug that one, I find myself in a room about twenty square feet. In the center sits a highbacked chair of green leather, rolling on casters, an exact duplicate of the chair Uncle Frank has in his office at the main house, though like everything else in the building, it's covered in dust. On impulse, I sit in the chair, and as my eyes acclimate to the low light, I see that all four walls are covered with framed photographs, most of them in black and white, but a few in color. The array extends from about waist-high to head-high. Every single photograph is of a beautiful woman. The women are of all colors and ethnicities, dressed in many different styles. The backgrounds show that the photographs were taken in places as far-flung as Marrakesh and Geneva, Rio de Janeiro, and Hong Kong. In each and every image, the subject gazes seductively, lovingly, even beseechingly at the photographer.

I spend some time in that chair, swiveling around, taking it all in. A little while later, I'm sitting beside Uncle Frank at the lunch table. At the other end, his blind, senile wife, my Aunt Helen, is fed by a nurse's aide. There are other people at the table, Frank's children and grandchildren, and some of them talk to me. I engage them in conversation but what I really wish I had the balls to do is lean in and very quietly, privately, whisper in Uncle Frank's ear—he's pushing ninety but still mentally clear—that I have been to his conquest gallery, his secret room.

If I had, would he have told me that he is glad for the way he spent his life and that, alone at night, he has no regrets and will have none until the day he dies? Would he have told me that he lived exactly the life he wanted? Would he have said that the meaning of life is to accumulate wealth, influence, and power and use it to "have" beautiful women, as well as rare and coveted goods? Though he shunned celebrity, adulation, and cultural notoriety, would Great Uncle Frank have confessed that the purpose of accumulating all that is to be able to "have" beautiful women along with rare, coveted, and collectible goods? Or might he have allowed that there is, in all of us, a completely different, secret yearning—one that has nothing to do with either experiences or possessions? Might he have told me that there was another project one could pursue instead, namely the deeper appreciation of the Way of Nature and the cultivation of the self? Might he have confessed to wishing he could be more like Master Po than the old man with his dusty downstairs portrait gallery? Probably not, but I sure do find myself more and more convinced that Po's path—romanticized, television monk though he may be—is going to be a better fit for me.

———————

Everyone wants to go to Yale. I realize what a great university it is, and what a great opportunity I have been given. The problem is, I'm just not cut out for school. Every day is like sliding down a razor blade into a bucket of alcohol, and choosing a major is like picking a finger to amputate. I pick Russian because I love my grandparents so much. They won't be around for long, their English is poor, and I love to hang with them and talk to them in their native tongue. I love the fiction too: Dostoevsky and Tolstoy, Lermontov and Gogol, Chekhov and Pushkin, Turgenev and Bulgakov. Trouble is, my brain just does not do well wilting in the steam heat of old New England buildings, sitting for hours in a chair listening to someone talk at a blackboard. I'm built to move, change the subject a thousand times in an hour, circle around to things, and nibble subjects like a rat at a pizza crust, taking my time to ingest the whole thing and do it my way. I get along with a syllabus and a classroom like I get along with sulfuric acid face scrub.

At the end of my last semester at Yale, SR, a young professor in the Russian Department, has a proposition for me.

> *I hear you're a backgammon shark.*
>
> *I enjoy the game.*
>
> *Well, I think I have a way for you to graduate after you fucked up your thesis.*
>
> *I didn't fuck it up. I just wrote something my advisor didn't like.*
>
> *Spin it however you like but you're looking at another semester here unless you help me out.*
>
> *I'm listening.*
>
> *There's this Israeli professor visiting the department.*
>
> *I know him.*
>
> *He's a backgammon shark, too.*
>
> *I had no idea. I've never played him.*
>
> *I'm into him for a few thousand. Win it back for me and I'll talk your advisor into letting you get out of here. You do want that, right?*
>
> *Desperately.*

The backgammon gambit unfolds at a graduation party at SR's house. The whole thing is a setup designed to get me to earn back SR's money. I have not met the Israeli until he shows at the party and SR casually brings us together.

> *Hey. I hear you two both like backgammon.*

I end up across the board from the guy and act surprised.

I had no idea!

The vodka starts flowing right away. This is great news for the Israeli but not for me. He is older, heavyset, an old hand at boozing; I'm a guy with a weak constitution—frequently ill, unable to withstand cold wind or water, sensitive to environmental allergens like dogs, cats, pollen, and mold. I have a heart that starts galloping after a single sip of booze.

And we do more than sip. We guzzle so much so fast, I'm not exactly sure which one of us has been suckered. The Israeli is a sharp player, and to me, the whole board looks fuzzy. I move my pieces as best I can, but backgammon is a game of statistics-based strategy. In the long term, strategy should win out, but in the shorter term…well, there are dice. SR sees me fading, plies me with pickles and black bread, and whispers in my ear.

To soak up the booze.

I use tricks to stay sober. I watch people come and go, count the number of lamps lit in the old Connecticut house. I read the Russian titles of piles of books on the shelves. There are some oriental rugs on the floor. They are threadbare but once they had color, like a lot of what I see in New England, save in autumn. I look at the bare patches, close my eyes, try to remember and envision them, and open my eyes again. Anything and everything to maintain focus and awareness rather than slip off into a boozy dream.

We play for hours. I calculate that the longer the game goes on, the worse it will be for me, as I'm going to pass out before the Israeli does. The wee hours of the morning arrive and pass. My classmates are strewn around, a handful of hardcore backgammon fans standing by me, others sprawled in chairs, a couple of future Masters of the Universe asleep on the floor. Close to dawn, the game tally approximates what I have to earn to graduate. Trouble is, we are neck and neck, this Israeli guy and I, and the way the game goes, everything can be won or lost in a single roll of the little white cubes.

We work the strategies and the odds, blocking and peeling, striking and guessing. We throw the dice in cups, challenging each other by upping the stakes, accepting, declining, starting a new round. The tick tock of a carriage clock on the mantelpiece is deafening. Embers crackle in the fireplace. A few people snore on chairs. The Israeli's eyes are rimmed red and magnified through his thick glasses. SR hovers like a hummingbird. We are in the thousands of dollars now—not my money, of course, but my undergraduate degree.

I get a run of luck. My mouth goes dry and I ask for water. The Israeli pours me vodka instead, pins me with a stare, and toasts me so I can't decline the drink. A few more rolls of the dice and we each have only a handful of pieces left on the board; the object of the game being to get rid of them all. The last roll comes. I see two fours and win with a grand flourish. Even the cat-nappers bolt up. SR punches the air. The embers suddenly roar into fire, perhaps because we have stirred the room with our exultations. Wait, says the Israeli. That was a three and a four, not two fours. I win. You lose.

My friends gasp. The dice have already been scooped up. No evidence remains. The outcome is one man's word against another's. SR jumps like he has his toe in an electric socket. Somebody turns on the lights, as if doing so will illuminate the truth. I'm a good thinker, sometimes even a deep thinker, but I'm not a fast thinker. In this case, however, raw need spurs me. Nonsense, I shout, it was double fours. Don't be a sore loser! Yeah, everyone cries, don't be a sore loser. A moment later, the Israeli bows to pressure and I graduate, not entirely sure who was right about the dice. I can't help but see a pair of far *larger* dice at work in my life. I wonder about chance. I wonder about fortune. I wonder about the random role of invisible forces in my life. I wonder what Master Po would say.

———·———

Diploma in hand, I have done what is expected of me by my family and am now free to find my own way in the world. I secure a job that starts in the fall, but I have the summer off. My parents kindly gift me a trip to the Galapagos Archipelago in celebration, against all odds, of having completed four years at Yale. The islands belong to the nation of Ecuador and lie six hundred miles off her coast in the Pacific Ocean. Tourist regulations require that before visiting the islands, I spread some cash around the capital city of Quito. At my hotel, I meet another guy who is in my highly regulated tour group. He is a herpetologist from Kansas and has the room next to mine. For him, as for me, this is the trip of a lifetime. At the hotel pool, I notice a pretty girl swimming laps in the pool beside me. I try not to stare at the way her thick blonde hair nests heavily against her creamy neck when she pauses to rest. I fail. She notices and gives me a smile. She tells me her name is E and that she is the daughter of the hotel manager. I offer to buy her dinner if she will show me a bit of the town.

E is fashionably late and makes an entrance, descending the sweeping hotel staircase like Vivien Leigh in *Gone with the Wind*. We take a long cab ride to a typical steakhouse with a woodburning oven. There is a brown concrete floor and blocky, country-style chairs and tables. Latin men in hats apply gaucho knives to flanks of barely-cooked cattle. E is charming, nervous, and engaging. We talk for hours, though I can't say about what. We laugh, we eat, we talk. We end up closing the place. I pay the bill and we leave the restaurant. Outside, we are at 10,000 feet, and I'm tired and lightheaded from the altitude. We cannot find a taxi, and in fact I don't see anyone another soul on the street. Hailing from Manhattan, I am confused.

> *Where is everyone?*
>
> *There isn't much nightlife under our ruling military junta. People don't stay out late these days. My apartment is much closer than your hotel. Would you like to go there?*
>
> *Great idea.*

The thin air is cool, and the pavement is cobblestone. Townhouses loom like gravestones against a starry sky. Each house is girded by a wrought-iron gate, and behind each lurks a jackal-eyed dog, narrow of snout, yellow of eye, and trained on us as if it knows we are alien: E, half-Swiss, and I from far to the north. E's stiletto heels flatter her legs but they are a grind on the cobblestones, birthing a raw heel before long.

> *Are you all right?*
>
> *I'll change out of these shoes as soon as we get home.*

Just then, a squat fellow in a forest-green uniform bumbles toward us. E looks suddenly nervous.

That's an immigration policeman.

So?

There's a ten o'clock curfew for foreigners.

You tell me this now?

I wanted to go out with you. And I never imagined we'd run into this guy in this neighborhood. Those guys never come here. Anyway, don't worry. Just don't say anything. Pretend you don't speak Spanish. I'll talk.

The cop's nametag identifies him as Luis Rivera.

He wants to see your passport.

I left it at the hotel.

I told him he's making trouble for nothing, but he insists. He just wants a bribe.

Clouds of rum emanate from the man, and he wobbles so violently, it appears he might tip. Reluctantly, I reach for my wallet. Just then, Rivera lunges forward, both hands aimed at E's breasts. It has been years since I watched a kung fu movie and even longer since I was mugged on the streets of Manhattan. Even so, I haul back and hit him, and he falls hard into the gutter.

The cobblestones are an unkind place to land. His head hits hard and he ends up facedown in shallow, moving water. He moves, but not much. Unwilling to wait for him to wake up, I grab E's hand and we start running. We have no plan other than to stay away from the streets, so we duck into an alley. The dogs apparently have been waiting for us, interlopers that we are, and they bark as we pass each front yard, pinpointing our location as surely as the finger of God. E breaks a heel. She can't run on the sharp stones, so I pick her up and carry her. I'm disoriented and the altitude robs me of my breath. I think we might be safe until we turn a corner and find the battered cop waiting for us.

This time, he has a revolver in hand. He points it at us, steps forward, and presses it to my temple. He smiles when he pulls back the hammer. The entirety of my attention, cosmically rich in this circumstance, constricts like the iris of a lens entirely focused on the round inch where the barrel meets my flesh. Vaguely, distantly, I notice the raw stench of his body odor. He marches me to a commandeered vehicle, a VW Type 3 Squareback, driven by some hapless local passerby. He forces both of us inside.

We drive in silence to the police station. Once we arrive, Officer Luis Rivera exits the vehicle, the revolver dangling from his finger. Heading in, presumably for reinforcements, he leaves us behind. I immediately turn my attention to the innocent driver.

Go!

He answers, looking genuinely rueful. It seems he knows what's about to happen all too well and knows there's nothing he can do about it.

I can't, I'm sorry. You're a tourist. I live here. If I leave, he will hunt me down, even if it takes him a year. He'll find me. He'll harass my family. He'll ruin my life. It will be a matter of pride for him. Of his reputation.

You're worried about machismo? He's dead drunk. He won't remember any of this.

He will remember everything.

Exasperated, I open the door and step out. There is no sign of Rivera. It's still the middle of the night, so the entrance to the station is quiet. Stricken, E hyperventilates. I grab her hand and once again we run. We are more successful this time. The dogs still bark and point us out, but we make significant headway in the direction of my hotel. Around four o'clock, we enter a square and need to cross it. Suddenly, floodlights bloom, changing the scene to something right out of François Truffaut's *La Nuit Américaine*. Spotlights mounted on Jeeps pin us down and soldiers surround us, pointing rifles. A portly young man saunters over. He is all in black, with jackboots and a swagger stick tucked under his arm. A real Nazi stormtrooper: although he looks to be a teen, I am later told he is twenty-one. E is terrified and whispers in my ear.

Military police.

The stormtrooper smiles and addresses me in good English.

> *So nice to finally meet the foreigner who has eluded us for so long. Please don't mistake me for that bungler Rivera, the one who left you in a car at the station. My name is Captain Romero. You assaulted an officer. You and I have so much to discuss.*

Romero forces E and me into the rear seat of a Jeep and assumes the spot by the driver. He levels a .45 Colt pistol at me as casually as licking apple pie from his fingers, then gestures for two more officers to climb on board beside us, half out of the vehicle, their machine gun barrels poking our sides. We are driving at high speed, in the cold and the dark, up toward mountain peaks illuminated only by starlight,

Captain Romero takes no chances. We leave the 10,000-foot city a glimmering carpet in the distance, which means we are at a nosebleed altitude, almost high enough to need oxygen, at least if you are not used to it. During the ride, desperate enough to try anything, I propose a deal with God. It's not a promise of obeisance but something else.

Get us out of this alive and I will learn how to hit a guy so he stays down.

There is no response.

Our destination is a mountain eyrie—Romero's personal hellhole, a concrete bunker where the young officer is free to exercise his will and power, unfettered and unwatched. I'm unceremoniously dumped into a cell with a dirt floor. A soldier follows me in and does things to me. After he leaves, I notice that another man is against the wall in the dark, and a third one is hidden in the flickering yellow shadows from a lightbulb near the door. I employ my best Spanish.

Come near me and die.

They stay away. Later, when a knife of dawn light filters through a narrow slit in the wall, cockroaches appear, a whole seething mass of them moving across the dirt to their daytime retreats. I can't imagine what they find so attractive about the cell—there is no food or water—but they are an expeditionary force and they distract me from E's not-so-distant cries.

After some time, I leave the safety of my corner to use the corner as a toilet. My cellmates are revealed to be thin, grizzled men whose expressions says they have been here before, know what is going to happen next, and will be here again. Their trousers are greasy and covered with the red dust from the floor. One of them wears a red and white bandana around his neck. Neither have hats. Both have of thick black hair. They won't look at me, for which I'm grateful.

More time passes. No food, no water. A day. Maybe another. A night comes and goes, but these are not the familiar quiet hours that grant me sweet sleep and memorable dreams but rather a tense, fraught, interval during which I feel absolutely anything could happen. At length, out of the late-night darkness a soldier appears and drags me to Romero's small office. E is there beside a desk and under a window, looking ragged and desperate, the buttons on her blouse broken. Romero sees me looking at her and smirks.

Are you alright?

Romero interrupts.

She's fine. Perfect. She has never been better.

I want to talk to her alone.

Romero smiles again and gestures with his hand.

Be my guest.

I wait until the door has closed behind him to speak to her.

Are you alright? I heard you screaming. What did he do?

What do you think?

I don't know what to say. She fills my silence.

I did what I had to do to survive. Please, can you get us out? You have to do it right now! The longer we remain here the more likely we will never leave.

Romero comes back.

My father is a powerful man with powerful friends. You're going to find yourself hunted down. Who knows what they will do to you when they find you? What I'm sure of is that you'll regret the day you were born.

On and on I blather, until Romero has finally had enough.

How much can you pay?

I'm not carrying cash, but I can give you American Express Travelers Cheques. They're in my hotel room. You'll have to take us back.

He rubs his fingers together in the universal gesture.

No checks. Only cash.

We haggle over a price and eventually reach an agreement. Once more, we are in an open Jeep but this time heading back down the mountain. E huddles against me. I amaze myself by thinking about Po. I rue how far away I am from China, which is a first. I rue how far away I am from being Po, too. That feeling, as much as anything that is going on, hurts me.

In the week hours of the morning, we pull up at the hotel—not at the front, but at the rear entrance. Another alley. The captain puts his big pistol not at E's temple but right against the center of her forehead.

If you want her to live, don't be long. And don't tell or bring anyone.

I make it to my room, retrieve the traveler's checks, and go to the front desk to cash them.

I need to cash these right now.

The cashier is not available at this time.

Your boss's daughter is outside in the alley. A military
policeman has a gun to her head and is waiting for the cash.

The clerk pales and flees, locking himself in a little room off the side of the desk. I can't believe it, but of course this is a country run by tyrants. I pound on the door. The clerk won't open it. Suddenly, I remember the herpetologist from Kansas, the one who is in my tour group to the Galapagos. I go upstairs and bang frantically on his door. He answers in a stupor, his belly tumbling over his BVDs, a Stetson lopsided on his head as it's the only thing one really needs to wear greet a stranger at the door at three o'clock in the morning. I am breathless, nearly incoherent.

They have E in a Jeep outside. We had a date. The police...
We were just walking down the sidewalk...drunk...
grabbed her. They want more cash to set her free. Don't
have enough...

He stares at me for a moment and then simply hands over his wallet. When you look up "prince of a guy" in the dictionary, there is this stranger's picture. I take the cash down to the alley and, warily, the captain and I do some business. Once E and I are free and back in my room, I call my father. He makes some calls of his own and within a few hours, I'm at the US Embassy. I tell my story and identify the perpetrators. There are some proceedings, during which time I offer to fly back down and testify in court if the men are brought up on charges. E is asked if she will do the same, but she declines.

I live here. This is my reputation. If I say anything, I'm a
ruined woman.

During my remaining time in this country, thanks to the intervention of the US State Department, I'm shadowed by a couple of guys in fedoras and trench coats wherever I go. I'm reminded of *Casablanca* and I'm grateful for it. The deal I made with a higher power is never far from my mind.

———·———

In the Chinese battlefield martial art of tai chi, we say: to go left, first go right; to go down, first go up. In the end, I will go as far east as a man can go without being on his way back, but first I go to Santa Barbara, California, a place I visited and fell in love with during my undergraduate years. I find a cheap apartment and enroll in some zoology courses at the university there. The bargain I made for my freedom from jail, not the payment to Romero but the *bigger* deal, is still on my mind so I enroll in a nearby Korean martial arts school rung by a champion named David Jang. He's the kind of guy who will line up his students front to back and then show off with a flying side kick, passing over all our heads like Bruce Lee, his movie-star coif fluffed, one callused foot extended, the other tucked to his knee, his hands balled in fists. There is a vague scent of limey Gillette aftershave as he goes by and I notice, with some satisfaction, a faint vertical line of sweat on the seat of his trousers. Bruce Lee is reputed to have had his sweat glands removed so as to look pristine for the camera and seem godlike in his effortlessness. Master Jang has not.

At the start of class, we line up in front of him. We all wear white cotton uniforms starched to such stiffness that they snap every time we move. One of the senior students, a tall, good-looking Mexican guy named Juan, produces a pair of weathered cowboy boots and holds them aloft like tournament trophies, a pair of Holy Grails, frank objects of worship. He kisses each one on the toe. These saved my life last night, he says, in a bar. Bunch of guys all at once. Spinning wheel kick. They're sorry now. Listening to this, I'm impressed. I have a pair of boots but they are shorter and only for walking in the mud, rain, and snow. I have never kicked anyone with them. This is because I have short legs and a long torso, both consequent to the overuse of corticosteroids to treat my childhood asthma. For me, a high kick comes up to another guy's navel. This deficit, which I try to ignore in daily life, can't be ignored in a Korean martial arts class. Even so, I press on.

Jang calls my apartment when I don't show up at class. Why you no down here? he screams into the phone. I have played hooky to study for exams but make it a point to miss as few classes as possible to fulfill my end of that heavenly bargain and at least learn to punch. I'm tired a lot. I study late into the night but don't want any more phone calls, so I come to class anyway. Just one time, a yawn sneaks out of me while he talks. He notices.

Am I boring you?

No sir. Was up late last night studying for an exam I had today.

Well, let's see if we can make class more interesting for you.

He tells me to sit down with my back against the wall. He puts the soles of my feet together, rests his hands on my shoulders, and suddenly jumps up and lands on the inside of my knees. My groin bursts into flame. I hear the tendons tearing, the muscles ripping. I see stars.

*I see that I now have your attention. Good to have you
here with us.*

He does not mention that this is a so-called special technique for opening the hip adductors, and that the next requirement is to keep stretching for weeks through the pain. Absent this information, I lick my wounds at home until the pain subsides, at which point scar tissue forms, and I'm even more inflexible than before. In pursuit of learning to fulfill my commitment and learn to hit a man so he stays down, it's pretty clear I'm not finding anything at all of Master Po, despite the fact that the name of Jang's art means "way of the Chinese fist" in Korean. Feeling a bit of a skulk, I find another school.

This one is better, at least for me. It is more American—something called American Kenpo, put together by a big Hawaiian guy, Ed Parker, who allegedly cherry-picked the best techniques from around Asia then came home from war or travel or both. I'm rube enough to buy the marketing here: the calendar on the wall has a new tourist photo of China for each month, a little plastic red pagoda with yellow strings sits in the window, some plastic frames on the wall represent all the material—that's the word for techniques—required to win a series of multicolored belts on the long climb to black. I'm hoping that even absent any actual Chinese or Japanese or Okinawan culture whatsoever, there is still something Master Po-ish about wearing a heavy cotton uniform and learning how to avoid getting beaten.

The whole movement thing is not really my bag. Well, it is, and it isn't. On the one hand, it makes me feel surprisingly good and provides a sense of kinship, especially after a long, hot class with lots of sweating, perhaps a split lip or a bruised rib, followed by a trip across the street with another student for some grocery-store Gatorade. On the other hand, I discover I well and truly suck at it. I'm an uncoordinated bumbler, probably consequent to my genetics and the first couple of decades of my life spent sucking asthma inhalers, missing gym class to lie in bed gasping for air. I can't throw or catch a ball or run more than a few yards without wheezing. My brain never really had a chance to wire itself to the body in my case; frankly put, connections are missing. I look at the ease of other students who see a move and copy it, and I'm struck by a combination of envy and despair. What I do have going for me, though, is persistence. I'm the guy who will repeat something five thousand times until, eventually, I get it right.

And I have one other asset. Maybe characteristic is a better word. I like to fight. I see weaknesses and how to exploit them to my advantage. This makes me rather good at mixing it up despite my shortcomings. It's a talent that causes me a Po-like angst—indeed, in my later corporate life, I will come to loathe it about myself—for it seems antithetical to hearing the crickets from afar and having a peaceful life in harmony with nature. I have an admittedly confrontational streak, perhaps Holocaust outrage rising in me, but I don't like to be told what to do by anyone, nor be forced to submit or yield. I really do learn a lot about myself from training in martial arts. Sadly, I find myself far from the person I hoped I would be.

———

Why don't I go to China and become Po right at this time? It's a question worth asking, and the answer is that it's neither politically nor logistically possible. More, my quest has not yet become a sharp enough blade for me to see my way to such a leap. I know I'm after equanimity and freedom, and I realize that both are a state of mind. What my ADHD brain can manage in this area, since I struggle with formal meditation, is to generate theta brain waves by riding a motorcycle down a country road. Other guys seem addicted to adrenaline; I'm addicted to a calm mind. I'm less interested in going fast than I am in savoring the feeling of zooming down the tarmac like a low flying bird, part of nature and the world, totally focused on the sensations in my hands and feet and in the need to pay survival-level attention. I have a great memory of riding my bicycle as a kid in upstate New York and zooming down into a fog-covered gully, having my bottom half disappear from view. On a motorcycle, this feeling is all the keener, more exhilarating, more complete. Rather than going as fast as possible on Southern California mountain roads, I try to prolong and intensify my state of mind, to see how far I can ride in a day, what new vistas and fragrances and nature I can find.

My favorite rides are east of San Diego, out to Julian and Mount Pinos by way of El Centro and the Anza Borrego Desert. I love the solitude, the self-reliance, the simplicity, the unburdening of my cares. I love the sense of having a destination, but even more, I love the sense of not having one, of chasing twisting roads and beautiful scenery rather than pursuing updrafts or prey. In one case, I ride up into Arizona, a journey of more than eight hundred miles that leaves me sore but with a great sense of having overcome odds, avoided danger, and having had a real adventure.

It's not what I have imagined, but right here and right now, motorcycling has some spiritual content for me. While still attending school in Santa Barbara, I ride an underpowered vintage BMW east across the country. I zig and zag on blue highways, prolonging the journey by going all the way north, then south again, never going very fast, making a fine journey out of it. Outside of Kalispell, Montana, I rise early and leave the comfort of a cheap motel toward a dark-as-night horizon. Just as the first fist-sized raindrop hits my visor, a highway patrol car crests a rise going the other way. We pass so close, we can see each other's faces. The officer shakes his head. I turn around and head back to the motel, trying to outrace the storm. I bring my bike up under the eave as the window shutters start to shake and the wind knocks over trashcans. I slip back into my room and watch The Weather Channel all day.

The next morning all is clear. On a whim, I change my plans and ride to South Dakota to see Mount Rushmore. I take refuge in a McDonald's, huddle in a booth with my gear piled high beside me and pull out Sogyal Rinpoche's translation of *The Tibetan Book of Living and Dying*. An underlying presumption of this classic Tibetan text is that we are reborn over and over again in an endless cycle called *samsara*. We may come back as roaches or eagles or people—this fate is the result of our *karma*, a tally of the pluses and minuses, the merits and demerits, our decisions and actions have earned us along the way. To escape this wheel of suffering, we must approach life a certain way, learn certain lessons, and make certain choices at the moment of death. The correct choices, and the incorrect ones, have been discovered by monks who have, over the course of millennia, explored the boundary between life and death through esoteric meditation. The more I understand about the profundity of the book I hold in my hands, the more imperative it seems to memorize the actions required to be free of the suffering cycle, right at the point of death. Knowing that I face death so closely by riding a motorcycle, I resolve not to leave the McDonald's until I have fully integrated the formula to escape to *nirvana*, some approximation of Heaven, should I be hit by a truck or lose control in the storm.

I'm caught in a serious summer storm whilst crossing a Minnesota levee. A gray curtain descends and the lights of the eighteen-wheelers ahead of and behind me fade. The water from the surrounding reservoir rises above my axles. My brakes fail and my already dim, old headlight vanishes into the rain. The plastic visor on my helmet fogs. I wipe it over and over with a soaking, black leather glove. I fear I will be run over before anyone even knows I'm there. I curse the steady drip of cold water defeating my collar and trickling down my back. I curse the ride. I curse the weather. I become more and more miserable. And then, suddenly, it occurs to me that I'm so lucky to be riding and engaging the elements in this gritty way. I can barely see, which just makes me feel like Po. My equilibrium returns. I change my mood and my perspective. Shifting in my seat, feeling the water slosh under my suit, I start laughing. Then I start singing at the top of my lungs; I hum Dylan tunes, pop songs from the Doobie Brothers, and the Eagles. My helmet becomes a private concert hall with an appreciative audience. I find a laundromat, dry my clothes, and sing away.

Continuing east, I decide to go visit my brother Stephen at his island home on the Outer Banks of North Carolina. The closer I get, the more signs I see referencing an impending hurricane. I've ridden a long way and the destination is a good one, so I hole up in cheap motels at night (rough neighborhoods are ok, but no bedbugs and nothing close enough to railroad tracks that shake the bed when a train goes by) and watch the progress of the storm, hoping it makes a turn before we meet.

Speeding toward the Ocracoke ferry that will take me out to the island, the edges of the monster system appear as saw-toothed clouds and wind. I'm calculating that I find shelter with my brother before the thing actually hits. I ride through water as high as the horizontally-jutting cylinders of my Bavarian machine. I make it as far as the loading ramp to the boat when men in yellow slickers come out and tell me, along with everyone in the line of cars behind me, that the ferry won't take passengers east. They are sending the boats over empty now to evacuate the island. I call Stephen from a payphone and learn that my gamble has failed and he himself is heading inland as the storm has grown and the ocean surge may destroy his place. I'm in a pickle now and thankful I finished Sogyal Rinpoche's book. I go through the death instructions in my mind, then pause at a payphone booth long enough to look up motels in the guidebook I have brought with me without getting the pages soaked. I call one after the other, looking for shelter from the storm. Not easy to find. Everyone on the coast has the same idea. Eventually, I drive as far inland as Asheville to find a room. The night manager lets me bring my bike into the motel lobby.

—————·—————

The ride over, I'm back to classes in Santa Barbara. My professor loves to work in the field. Catching animals and throwing them into jars of formaldehyde, sometimes still alive for a horrible, burning death, is not my cup of tea any more now than it was when I trapped and shot animals in Paraguayan Chaco. It seems a morally dubious thing (I'm being kind here, as it's obviously outrageous) to take lives in order to satisfy our curiosity about a family tree or genetic variations in a lizard population and so on. I begin to get the feeling that a lot of the guys I meet in this academic pursuit just like to be paid to walk around outside. What they surely do not see, but what is becoming increasingly apparent to me, is that there is narcissism in the sciences just as there is in the literary world. We just think too much of ourselves, particularly in relation to the rights and characteristics of species other than our own.

I don't yet know that Daoism, the religion/philosophy in which I will eventually become an ordained monk, is the first environmentalism, the first organized way of looking at the harmony and balance in Nature of which we are a part. What I do know is that slaughtering other living creatures in the name of science is not for me. I want to treat them with compassion, not kill them, so rather than pursuing a PhD in evolutionary biology, I shift my plan and apply to veterinary school. Admission is notoriously difficult, but I manage to get in a few places. Before I start, I have to satisfy a requirement for hands-on experience, so I apply for a research position at the San Diego Zoo, working in the reptile house. The job requires being exposed to dangerously venomous snakes. Treatment for a bite from those is with a serum derived from horses. My equine allergy is so strong that horse proteins injected into my bloodstream would probably kill me faster than the venom of any snake, so I choose not to mention the allergy. I get the job and move down to San Diego. Daily, I work with aptly named death adders and monkey-tail skinks. The zoo is amazing, though I can't avoid the abiding feeling that animals in cages live sad, deprived, and fractured lives— again to satisfy human urges. Here as at school and on a motorcycle, it is *always* the spiritual dimension of what I'm doing that takes center stage.

Now in a new town, I decide to build up on my experience in American Kenpo and try for my first black belt. I find a school run by Glenn Small, a young ex-Navy man, model-handsome, a lover of women, fast cars, alcohol, and bar fights in equal measure. He's no Po but his techniques are clear and strong. One day a lightbulb in the school ceiling burns out and he asks me to change it. This requires a climb all the way to the very top of a rickety stepladder. Nobody is spotting me and reaching up for the bulb the ladder nearly gives way. I manage to swap the bulb, but the job reminds me that I don't like heights. I notice him watching me through the office window.

When the time comes for my brown belt test, the one before black, he brings some Marines down from Camp Pendleton. The three of them wail on me for a couple of hours. I suffer a broken finger and a broken rib. One grabs me and the other kicks me in the face. I hear a crunching sound. Glenn breaks up the fight.

Hey. I want to get them back.

He shakes his head and gestures at the school closet.

Not now. Come with me.

I follow him into the little space where we keep a pail and mop, along with some uniforms, belts, and T-shirts. He puts his thumbs on either side of my nose.

Take a deep breath and then let it out.

I do. He slides his thumbs down my nose. I see a flash of light, feel another stab of pain, and hear another loud crunch.

What the hell was that about?

What was it about? Your nose was pointing east and the rest of you was pointing north.

My black belt test with Glenn is less traditional and far more alarming. As the day draws to a close, he asks me to meet him at eight thirty that Saturday morning. He tells me he has closed the school to regular classes that day. I am there early and wait for him in the parking lot; the appointed hour comes and goes. No sign of Glenn. One part of me thinks he's been out drinking and has forgotten my test, another thinks that the waiting is part of the game. I sit tight. At ten thirty, he rolls up in his black Corvette. He looks a bit ragged. He bids me to follow him to the edge of the shopping plaza that contains the school. The mall is surrounded on three sides by a twelve-foot-high wall made of concrete cinderblocks. The wall is shaped like a wide "u." On two sides, the wall separates the plaza from the sidewalk. On the third side, the long side bordering the alley behind the shops, the wall separates the plaza from a sheer drop into a steep California-desert ravine littered with cactus and boulders perhaps a hundred feet below.

We arrive at the front end of one of the two side walls.

Get up on the wall.

I look at him like he's joking, but he's not. He offers a boost with his clasped hands and up I go. Standing atop the narrow wall, I feel unstable, acrophobic, nervous. He begins to shout out the names of self-defense techniques, requiring me to balance on the wall and execute them. He follows along as I walk the wall toward the ravine. If I fall off on one of the short sides of the "u" I will break a leg. If I fall into the ravine, I will likely die. We get to that city-block-long wall and he demands a series of spinning kicks with jumps. I don't see how I'm going to survive this. I do the kicks. He barks out commands for form sequences, for punches, for blocks. I work my way long the wall until, by the end, I've lost eight pounds of water weight and I'm shaking all over.

The last leg of the "u" requires more techniques but at least I'm in a comparatively safe area now. When I reach the end, I'm so exhausted I can barely stand. We kneel facing each other on the hot asphalt of the parking lot and he presents my black belt and certificate to me right there. I've had many, many other rank tests in multiple systems since then, but never one riskier, crazier, and perhaps never one more rewarding.

I'm frequently alone on those San Diego weekends as I'm a transplant and I don't know anyone. One night, I stop by a video arcade, where a beautiful half-Asian woman plays Pac-Man by herself, serially rebuffing every guy who tries to engage her. I stare in amazement as she beats the machine time after time, setting one record after another. BA is a phenom, and everyone in the place knows it. I approach her, wait for her game to finish, and the moment it does, slip a quarter into the slot, funding the next round for her. She looks at me without a word and gets back to playing. The next time the game ends, I put two quarters in, and this time she chooses the two-player option. When my turn comes, I die in about ten seconds. She smiles, shakes her head, and goes back to working her magic. I hang around.

You're persistent.

I am.

Interesting. Most guys don't like to pay to get their asses handed to them over and over.

*Most girls get hungry after winning so much. How about a
drink and some dinner?*

Six months later, we are a married couple living in
Ithaca, where I matriculate at the New York State College
of Veterinary Medicine at Cornell University. I find the
memorization of the coursework burdensome but some of
the concepts interesting. My classmates are some of the
smartest and nicest people I've ever met. I even find time to
train in White Crane Kung Fu with an engineering student
from China, and in Shōrin-ryū weapons with a high-ranking
female black belt. I can't say I find Master Po in any of these
teachings, but I'm nibbling around the edges of Chinese
philosophy and culture by pursuing them.

In 1983, a few days before Christmas, BA and I caravan
downstate to see my parents. We are in two cars because
we bear dogs, snakes, turtles, and gifts. On that gray day
on a winding, snow-lined country road south of town, an
oncoming vehicle crosses the line and hits BA head-on at
a combined speed of over a hundred m.p.h. The accident
unfolds in seconds but I see it as a slow-motion film, a great
and sudden billow of snow, the sound like high-frequency
thunder, the ultraviolet atmosphere, invisible but merciless,
rendering every detail of crushed metal and pets, twisted
in a cyclone of impact, pawing unnaturally against the
grit of gravity, the sideways-skittered vehicles come to at
random angles. I run to the scene and find my sweet wife's
mangled face dangling out of what is left of the driver's
window, features askew as if grabbed and squeezed by the
ruthless hands of an unkind god. Strangers—passersby who
leap from surrounding cars—pull me away as traffic nearly
instantaneously piles up in both directions.

BA is airlifted to a regional hospital, barely alive, the stem of her brain, as is the given term, insulted. Swaddled in gauze, tubes from every orifice, she is bundled, strapped, and taken by ambulance to New York Hospital, where my father arranges a neurologist who has written a book on the phenomenon of coma to direct her care. I sleepwalk through my world, the details a blur, the disposition of my found dogs, my studies, my home, my clothes, all waves breaking unseen upon the beachhead of my abject despair. Days and weeks pass with me at BA's bedside while she clenches her fist to her chin and receives food and fluids through needles, her eyes closed, monitors beeping and chirping, and a steady round of nurses navigating through their dizzying routines of changed linens, medications administered, therapies exercised, and sponge baths given, the only real marker of the passage of time. I find myself thinking a great deal about fate, karma, Heaven, Hell, and Dao. More than that, I recognize a streak within myself that hasn't been so clear to me before, although I've sensed it. I don't really want to be *in* this world. I want to float above it and use it as an object lesson for bigger things. I don't really want to engage fully with anything other than the path to being Master Po. All else is a distraction.

This, it turns out, will always be so.

After a month, the coma expert calls me to his well-worn carpet. He has an office in the hospital, a secretary out front, wood paneling, a broad desk with two perching gooseneck lamps, and furniture in the stolid and uninspired style of the Doctor's Coat Room. He has lunch brought in for himself— crudité on a clear plastic tray—and he munches on it as I sit expectantly, my heart in my throat, waiting to hear the verdict on my wife.

Injuries like these don't resolve well. The scans show very little activity in her brain.

He dips a broccoli floret into some ranch dressing and brings it quickly to his lips. A drop of the dressing hits the blotting paper on his desk, and he dabs at it with a paper napkin. He picks up a carrot stick next, holding it aloft.

Bottom line is that this is your wife. Better get used to it. No miracle is coming.

She wakes up the next day. The nurses show me a note on her medical chart that reads: "miracle recovery." I'm overjoyed and confused at the same time.

The doctor said she'd forever be a vegetable.

The nurse rolls her eyes.

You think doctors understand why things like this happen? You'd be better off talking to a chaplain about it.

The tubes are quickly removed from BA's mouth and nose. It takes her a while to wake up after the scans normalize. When she sees me, she has no idea who I am. She does not know my name. She does not remember marrying me. She has no idea of a lot of other things, either, nor does she have the ability to stand or walk or perform routine tasks. She can't use one of her arms. The road before her is long and tortuous, agonizing, and very, very expensive.

Consequent to one instant of disaster, my spiritual quest is pushed aside by the gritty reality of taking care of a disabled wife. Whatever stubborn, self-centered certainty there is that something larger is going on has been simultaneously confirmed by a miracle, then set beyond my reach. My quest to pull back the veil of my senses and see what really is ends up in a dusty, distant corner of my mind. I'm now in service to nothing but BA's gigantic medical debt, the therapists, hospitals, doctors, nurses, medications, and more. I chip away at what I owe. I take care of my wife. I try to make vet school work, but I can't take care of her and do the classwork. I withdraw and move back to California so she can be closer to her family.

I make a little money by teaching martial arts, but not more than a little. There is no spiritual dimension to the arts as I do them, they are only a way to stay fit, strong, and healthy so that I can do what I need to do. Even so, I enjoy working with my students and I enjoy the rigors of the practice. My physical skills improve. I change styles, go back to a different sort of American Kenpo—a streetwise amalgam of different Asian styles—and gain an instructor's black belt. I find that I have a knack for teaching, so I open a franchised school.

When I'm not taking care of BA, I promote the business, practice, and teach. Between lessons, I write in the back office. My one indulgence is to take myself to a nearby sushi restaurant for lunch a few times a week. T, a striking Japanese-Irish waitress, befriends me. Her attentions flatter me. She comes by the school. She is interested in me but despite her charms, I explain that as lovely as she is, I cannot reciprocate.

> *I'm holding my life together by a thread. I have a handicapped wife at home. I have a huge medical debt to pay down. I have this school to run and I'm making a few bucks a day writing advertising copy for a local paper. If we start something, all I have will unravel.*

T understands but doesn't entirely give up.

One day, I get a call that the grandmaster of my Kenpo system—and the franchisor—wants to see me. I have never met the man and figure he is going to chew me out for not doing better with enrollment and earnings in my fledgling business. I don't fully understand then what I will understand later, which is that to make a martial arts school successful, you have to run a daycare for kids. Moreover, there will be very few serious students, and of those, only a tiny percentage who see their practice as a way to awakening the mind and spirit. And why would this not be so? I'm not living in ancient China, David Carradine's *Kung Fu* TV show is no more, and Bruce Lee is dead. I myself may enjoy Shaw Brothers martial arts movies featuring supernatural themes, exotic traditional weaponry, "wire-fu" stunts, Chinese nationalism, the warrior spirit, loyalty to teachers and systems and schools, and occasionally some shamanistic elements, but nobody can claim these have anything to do with reality.

The grandmaster's flagship school looks normal enough upon entry—mats, bags, cheap Asian artwork on the walls, the requisite red-tasseled swords on the walls, beaded door dividers, black, slotted privacy screens. There is lacquered artwork everywhere, highlighted in mother of pearl, rendering farmers with big sun hats and staffs in hand who push water buffalo alongside streams, and snow-capped mountains in the distance that make nature look grand and humans look small. Standing in stark contrast to the Western, Abrahamic notion of man's preeminence in the world, the humility suggested by such landscape paintings—a Chinese and particularly a Daoist tradition—puts man in his proper place as a miniscule cog in a giant, organic, everchanging, and fundamentally unknowable universe.

Entering the back office at the rear of the school, I find none of this humility in evidence. The grandmaster sits behind a desk like a human bullfrog. Four men flank him, two on each side. I know three of these guys by reputation, and have already met the other, as he has given me special street-fight training. They are soldiers, bruisers, thugs, scorpion escorts to the frog, each with a formidable sting but able to be swallowed in a gulp. They stare at me impassively, arms crossed. The frog looks at me without blinking.

My guys tell me you can rumble.

I want to tell him about Master Po the way I once wanted to tell my father about Eddie the doorman, but think better of it.

Actually, I'm more into the philosophy. And I really like to help people get healthy, get in shape, learn how to handle themselves.

The scorpions roll their eyes. The frog shakes his head, reaches under the desk, produces an attaché case, and plops it down on the desk. I recognize a Halliburton briefcase; I have one like it at home. Some years earlier, landing at Denver Airport, two undercover cops in Hawaiian shirts and shorts approached me, flashed badges, and asked to look inside the one I was carrying. Turns out, couriers favor the brand for the way the O-ring seal keeps drug smells from dogs.

The bullfrog pushes the case toward me.

Take this case to Chicago. Someone will meet you at the airport. Give it to him and get the next flight back.

What's in the case?

The question hangs in the air like a cloud of nerve gas. The scorpions advance, their poisoned tails lifted high and pointed in my direction. The bullfrog answers me.

That's not your concern.

Forgive me, Grandmaster, but if I'm carrying something I have to know what it is.

The scorpions take another step forward. I can hear them breathing. I have to say something else quickly, and I do.

Regardless of the case and its contents, I can't leave town. I'm the caregiver for my handicapped wife. She needs constant attention. Traveling isn't an option. A few hours away for this meeting was all I could manage.

The bullfrog does not like this answer at all, and glances at his scorpions, disgusted.

Is this true?

The smallest and deadliest of the arachnids offers a nod.

You knew this and still set up the meeting? What a waste of time.

I start to edge backward toward the door, mumbling.

I'm sorry I let you down, Grandmaster.

On the way home to look after BA, I wonder how I could have been so naïve as to get professionally involved with mobsters recruiting enforcers and couriers from the ranks of their own martial arts schools. Master Po, I'm certain, would not approve.

I'm twenty-nine years old and the money I make teaching martial arts doesn't even keep pace with the accrual of interest on BA's massive financial debt. It's bad enough that I'm going backward on the financial treadmill, and my own training time—along with any access to Master Po and the spiritual realm—are supplanted by trying to be a good teacher and meet the needs of others. I'm alone in this pursuit, indeed I'm entirely alone in my life, as my marriage has turned into a caretaking relationship. This is nobody's fault, save perhaps that of the driver who crossed the center line on that wintry country road, and BA's suffering utterly eclipses my own. All the same, there are times I need a break.

Writing fiction provides it. Novel-writing allows me to create worlds as I would have them rather than how I live them. While I might not be on the path to becoming Master Po, the act of writing drives the material world so far into the background, it no longer seems relevant or real. My concentration is so intense that any sudden noise or movement sets my heart pounding, and a larger disruption makes me feel anxious, nauseated even, almost as if I have been yanked from a dream. All day long I wait for this escape. Writing deprives me of sleep, but I feel I am finally living up to my potential. My first novel, *Triggerman*, sells to a major New York publisher in exactly six days. It does not make as much money as my previous title, the nonfiction work *Exotic Pets*, but it's well-received for a first effort and I start planning a second one.

In the meantime, I continue to pen advertising copy, no longer for the local circular but for small local companies, and then for a Dallas-based corporation that manufactures and distributes high-grade nutritional supplements called nutraceuticals—referencing that they can function as medicines, in specificity and potency, and that they are manufactured to pharmaceutical standards. The first project for this company is a corporate brochure. I have never had a corporate client before and I charge a lot for the job. They are happy with it and give me more to do: sales materials, product brochures, guides to weight loss and performance products that include multivitamins, antioxidants, and sports drinks. I write the copy, they pay the money, which goes directly to paying BA's bills.

The company tells me my material has become so important to them that they want the sales force to thank me in person at their annual meeting in Dallas. I tell them my wife is incapacitated and I can't leave her. In response, they arrange for special transportation, accommodation, and onsite nursing care for her. We fly to Dallas. Before the sales meeting, I tour the company offices, putting faces to the names of people I have been working with by phone and mail. I may not have business experience, but I have instincts, and these reveal more sizzle than steak among the staff; still, I have been told a Nobel laureate in chemistry is on the board, along with sport and medical luminaries, and that the products are well-regarded and considered safe and effective.

The meeting is a spectacle. William Shatner, *Star Trek's* Captain Kirk, officiates in the ballroom of a nice hotel with gold curtains, linen tablecloths, and a well-catered meal with a choice of chicken filets sautéed in white wine and butter, sprinkled with parsley, or pork chops with Mexican mole sauce sided by mashed potatoes. There is an open bar, with lots of enthusiastic salespeople mingling with the company's big fish. The chairman makes a speech. He is a carnival barker with a bad toupee, but he gets the troops riled up. I'm up on stage for a few minutes and the sales force applauds me for helping them so much by writing good and useful sales tools. BA watches from a wheelchair.

Sunday morning, I'm preparing for the return trip when the house phone rings. The medical director and the chairman are downstairs. They want a breakfast meeting. I tell them I'm getting ready to fly, but the chairman insists.

Just a quick bite and a chat.

A few minutes later, I meet him in the hotel coffee shop. The chairman leads off.

You're smart. I can smell it. I want you to work for me full time here in Dallas.

I'm grateful for all the work you've give me and flattered by the offer. The thing is, my wife's family is in California, and I have other work there as well. I'm totally delighted to keep doing a great job for you, though.

What other work?

I run a martial arts school and I do other copywriting jobs. I also write novels.

There's no future in retail and no cash in fiction. The future is now. Here. With me. With this company. Don't blow it.

We spar back and forth. My character defects and his come to the fore; I don't like to be bullied and he won't be denied. The more I demur, the harder he presses. At length, I realize my lucrative writing job is over. I try to console myself with the ad writing experience I have gained. I can do this for other companies, I think, and while I do, I can work on that second novel. The chairman sees he is losing me and presses harder, going so far as to push my food out of the way and lean in. That is the last straw for me.

> *You want to know why I won't move here and work for you? The real reason?*
>
> *Sure I do.*
>
> *Because I've learned something spending days in meetings with you and your people.*
>
> *Is that right? What have you learned?*
>
> *That none of them is smart enough to be my boss.*

The medical director spits up his bagel. A sad and soggy white glob lands on the chairman's placemat. We all stare at it. The silence is excruciating. I wish I could suck my words back down my throat, but before I can dig a deeper hole, the chairman starts laughing.

> *I'll be goddamned if that isn't the truth.*

He turns to the medical director.

> *Didn't I tell you he was smart?*

The director pushes himself back from the table, his fingers splayed wide. He doesn't seem to have anything to say, but the chairman isn't done.

> *How about this? How about you move here, and I make you the boss?*

The medical director takes to his feet. His face is red. The chairman mentions a salary no part-time copywriter, precious few novelists, and certainly no martial arts teacher could ever hope to earn. It's the proverbial offer and it will go a long way to paying off my bills. We shake hands and I fly home. A week later, a moving van arrives, and BA and I are off to Texas.

In the first year of the job, I osmotically absorb the principles and operations of business through skin made permeable by abject financial desperation. I reorganize a good chunk of the company, hire new staff, and dramatically increase sales. I climb the ladder there. Our products capitalize on the antioxidant theory of disease, which will be well accepted in the future but is cutting edge, perhaps dubious medicine now. We blur the boundaries between nutritional supplements and medications and are hounded by the FDA and the media for doing so. We employ celebrities like Shatner to endorse the products. Connie Chung leads a CBS News crew in an attempt to skewer us for unsubstantiated claims. Interviewing me, her cameraman shoots from the hip while swearing he is not filming. I'm sideways and unflatteringly rendered in the voiceover asking who is this man? They don't ask who this future monk is. Through all this, I find myself in denial of my boss' marketing excesses and overall shady character, but I don't doubt the quality and effectiveness of the products. I use them every day.

One Friday night, I work late at my new office, a frame and drywall cube right in the middle of the operations floor rather than in the executive building with other top brass among the fountains and high ceilings and marble floors. I'm alone in the place, tapping away on my computer, when I hear a noise that I should not be hearing so long after everyone goes home. I follow it to the loading dock, where our products are packed and loaded onto trucks for nationwide distribution. I find my boss's sidekick pitching pennies with the loading crew. He is a smarmy guy, always walking the company halls without a seeming purpose. He crouches like a Balinese cane cutter, heels on the floor, hips loose, brown suitcoat grazing the concrete. Around him, I see an array of open cardboard boxes filled with our products, cans of diet powder, plastic bottles of vitamins, and something else, something that should not be there—clear plastic bags filled with white powder. I immediately understand what is happening, why these men are here late, what the real job of this guy is. These men are using our shipping facilities to distribute street drugs across the country. Cocaine and maybe other things, too. In what could be a moment from a Hollywood thriller, the sleazy guy stares at me. I stare back. Not a word is spoken but I feel real menace. My bowels roil. I retreat to my office, quickly gather my things, and duck out the alleyway door to where my motorcycle waits.

I ride home, my mind full of the knowledge that my boss must know what is going on and be generating extra cash with this scheme, perhaps even profiting more from it than from the legitimate side of our business. I can't know. I spend a sleepless night beside my wife, my hand under my pillow, resting upon a Smith & Wesson Model 19, a .357 magnum revolver with a target hammer and trigger, a gun I'm good with, a gun I shoot regularly at the shooting range. First thing Saturday morning, I contact my attorney. We draft a letter to the *Dallas Morning News*. I sign it and leave it in his care.

I'm in my boss's office first thing Monday morning. He doesn't appear surprised to see me but touches his oversized glasses nervously and adjusts his ridiculous toupee. He waits for me to say something and I do.

> *We have a booming business. It may be cutting edge and controversial and we may get into trouble with our claims, but it's a legitimate enterprise and we have our customers' best interests at heart. We're trying to do some good in the*

world, help people feel better, stop them from getting sick. Not only that, but we have hundreds of people working for us in house. A great team. They're good people who try hard and do a great job, which you can see from the sales numbers alone.

Your team. Loyal to you.

I work for you. My team is your team. You're the boss. The problem is that now that I know what's happening on the loading dock, I can't stay quiet about it. I'm just not that kind of guy.

There's a pause. I can see he's thinking. Perhaps he's reflecting on our breakfast meeting and how he should have foreseen this moment, knowing what he did and what I did not. He's quiet for a while, then comes up with a disappointing reply.

I don't know what you're talking about.

I look down at the expensive cowboy boots I purchased with company funds after he shredded my Birkenstocks with poultry shears, in his kitchen, during a Super Bowl party. I take out a fancy pen the company bought me.

I'll go to the police, and you'll go to jail. Wouldn't it be a lot nicer to sail the Caribbean in your lovely lot for a few months? Put some distance between yourself and all this while I continue to grow our legitimate business and make you an even richer man?

He opens the drawer of his desk. My fear is that it will be a pistol. Instead, he produces a nail file. For a few moments, he is absorbed in manicuring himself. Then he looks up at me.

*I have people in New Orleans. My team. I mean my real
team. The Big Easy is not so very far from here. Those
people can be here quickly. Overnight. Faster than that.
Once they arrive, you disappear. You understand what I'm
saying? Nobody ever hears from you again. Not your wife,
your parents, your friends. Poof, you're just gone.*

I nod.

*I'm sad to say I expected this to be your answer, loving
the Big Easy the way you do. So I made some plans. I
disappear, the newspaper gets a letter. I have to call every
couple of hours and let them know that I'm safe until we
resolve this.*

I could force you to call.

Not every hour.

Sure I could.

*Yeah? And for how long. Anyway, there's a code word that
lets them know I'm safe.*

There is no such word, although I wish I'd thought to add
one. He considers for what feels like an hour, then finally nods.

I'm not going to do what you ask.

It's my turn to nod, and to withdraw a folded piece of
paper from my suit pocket.

I didn't think you would. So there's another option.

He grins broadly.

I've turned you into a businessman.

I push the paper across his desk. It outlines a generous
severance. One that will all but cancel out BA's debt. It's a

THE MONK OF PARK AVENUE

payoff and I don't feel good about it. I can see he doesn't love it either. I can almost hear the gears in his head running the cost/benefit analysis, assessing the risk, considering his Big Easy option, ruminating over what he has to lose.

> My bank account numbers are at the bottom. For the wire. I'll expect to see the full balance in the account before banking hours are over today.

I leave him holding the paper and stand up and leave. I go home. BA is already on a plane back to California to her family. There is a rented trailer attached to my car in the driveway. Revolver on my lap, I await a call from my bank to confirm a wire transfer. When it comes, I pack and close the trailer quickly, looking furtively around the whole time, in and out of the house, bringing only what I really care about. My African Grey Parrot, Greta, exits the house on my shoulder, where she remains for the drive west. Greta has been with me for years, even making a TV appearance on the *Gary Collins Show*, a variety show of the time, to demonstrate her four-hundred-word vocabulary. I put my pet snakes and turtles in the backseat and leave Dallas. Some months later, the Texas State Attorney General raids the company. Charges are filed. The company is sold and later declares bankruptcy.

The good work I do in Dallas does not go entirely unnoticed. In 1987, longtime family friends, the Sacklers, notice what I have done in Texas and ask me to come work for them in Connecticut. Their company is Purdue Pharma, manufacturer of antiseptics, laxatives, douches, ear washes, fiber crackers, a sustained release morphine sulfate compound, and, later, the infamous OxyContin. I sell my martial arts school and go to work for them.

This is a family business, originally a cocreation of three brothers. Two are left to run it as the third passes away. As they age, the remaining family scions are bitterly at odds over the succession plan for the company. Each wants his own children, his own vision for the company, to be the one that prevails. Their succession battles meld with greed and some sense of service to create a very particular corporate culture. The family is kind to me, helpful, supportive. They make me feel comfortable and I give them good creative work, though I worry that their fixation on serving the doctor rather than the patient is an elitist view. I see it as a part of the larger problem, namely that the American Medical Association has seen to it that allopathic physicians, the same folks who early on hawked snake oil from horse-drawn carriages, are now seen as gods. One result is that patients have abdicated responsibility for their own care, even their own lives. Propagating the fiction that we ought to rely on someone else to keep us healthy keeps this vast healthcare machine lubricated. Combined with Big Sugar, which has addicted us all, and both Big Agriculture and factory farming, which poison us daily, the cycle is complete. We are made sick, pay money to feel better, and made sick again. On and on it goes—with few of us ever stopping to think we can change it—as the doctors and the pharmaceutical and insurance companies get richer by the day.

I'm thirty years old and worried that Master Po would judge me harshly for being part of such a system, as he would lambast me for walking away from a drug-running scheme without blowing the whistle. I'm chagrined by my defects of character but resigned to accept at least *some* of the realities of the world. In truth, I enjoy the Purdue team, finding them to be supportive, smart, helpful, and friendly. I relish the creative challenges of reimagining Purdue's over-the-counter products, which include laxatives, antiseptics, douches, and more. I work on rebranding lines, changing packaging, and improving advertising. I'm given leave to hire agencies to represent the company. Interviewing firms in New York affords me to meet legends in the advertising business, to have lunch with George Lois at The Four Seasons, to overhear myself referred to as the "Lord of Laxatives" and the "Sultan of Shit" by some account managers. I find a boutique Greenwich Village agency, Holland Advertising, and give them the account. Holland reframes Purdue's products, focusing in particular on Senokot laxative and using the James Brown song *I Feel Good* to promise more than just success on the porcelain throne. The results are strong sales.

Making money, I'm willing to spend a little. I take BA on a trip to Australia, a place both of us have long wanted to go. There are some logistics involved—getting the medication right, making sure we have enough rest, some extra time needed for transportation—but all in all we both enjoy the trip. We see wallabies; BA loves wallabies. We see fantastic birds, mostly cockatoos. I have loved scuba diving since I was a kid, so we take a boat to Heron Island, a dive retreat on the Great Barrier Reef. Quarters are modest. Tin-roofed Quonset huts. Meals are communal. Nobody cares about food, other than eating enough of it. Diving makes you hungry. Even in the tropics, divers burn calories in the water trying to stay warm. BA is able to float above the reef wearing a mask and breathing through a snorkel and clutching my hand. She gets to see manta rays, eels, colorful fish, even small sharks. It's marvelous to see her so excited and so happy. It makes all the work and the wheeling and dealing seem worthwhile to me.

One night, after a day of three dives, two of them very shallow so I don't get the decompression sickness—known as the bends—the hotel manager lightly touches my elbow at dinner.

Sir. We have a satellite call for you.

A satellite call?!

That's all we have here. No wires or cables so it's for emergencies only.

My heart a Ferrari at redline, I go to the phone, which is heavy, yellow, and attached to a box with lights and a thick cord. I find the caller is my father.

Dad? Is everything all right?

No.

Are you ok? Is Mom ok?

Yes, but your Unk just came to see me in the office. I diagnosed him with terminal cancer. I think it might have to do with that toxic metal that made him his fortune. I haven't told anyone. I'm holding it in. I needed to tell someone.

I'm stunned by the fact that he would reach out to me across the world rather than speaking to someone closer.

How long does he have?

Not long. And his death is going to be a terrible thing.

There is a storm that night. Good thing the call got through when it did, at least for my father's sake, so he does not carry the pain by himself. Fig-sized raindrops on the tin roof are deafening, but not enough to drown out the moaning of the mutton birds in their burrows, a serenade that has been with us since our arrival, one of many eerie sounds on the bottom side of the world. In so many ways adrift, BA sleeps the sleep of the dead. She does every night; she takes barbiturates to stop her brain from seizing, a good thing as I have seen her seizures and never want to see her endure one again. I lie awake thinking about Unk, whom I love as much as I love anyone in the world. I can't bear the news, the prospect of his suffering, losing him from my life. I sit up in bed. With rain clouds over the moon and only a trickle of electricity available to each hut, the darkness is infinite.

Suddenly, something appears just off the foot of the bed—a greenish glow. I stare at it, reach over, and shake BA's shoulder. She does not stir. The glow intensifies, then takes on the form of a floating torso whose blurred edges sharpen to reveal my Grandfather Arthur. He is as I remember him, though not as wasted as he was at the end, as I saw him when I returned from Paraguay.

Grandpa?

You never think of me anymore.

Don't be silly. Of course I do.

Stop that. You can't lie to me. Not to any of us. We know everything.

I'm too afraid to ask what he means by we, so I pose another question altogether.

Where are you?

I can't tell you.

Why not?

Words don't work for this.

Well, are you in Heaven?

He shakes his head. The next question is much harder.

Are you in Hell?

He shakes his head again and the next answer comes in something of a whisper, at least his voice seems quieter than when first he spoke.

Death is different than you imagine. You could say
I'm in limbo.

Well, despite what you think you know, I do think of you. I
was just telling someone the story of how you and I were on
the Long Island Expressway in your beige Mercedes. Your
driver, Fred, was at the wheel and he took the wrong exit.
You yelled at him so hard he backed up the off-ramp to get
back on the road.

That Mercedes wasn't beige, it was dark green. Like a forest
at twilight.

Oh. Right. It was green. You wanna know something
funny? After you died, Fred became my dad's driver.
One time he was taking Dad and a world-famous
heart surgeon...

Mike DeBakey.

Right. They dropped DeBakey at his hotel, but what
they didn't know was that Debakey walked out another
entrance to the hotel to grab a paper and crossed the street
right in front of Dad's car.

Fred hit him.

This makes me laugh a little bit and glance over at BA, hoping that the conversation has awakened her. No luck.

Yes! How did you know?

I told you, we know things.

Dad jumps out of the car and runs up and helps DeBakey up. DeBakey looks at him as if Dad intended it, as if Dad thought the whole thing was funny. Dad sent Fred to the eye doctor. Turns out he's totally blind.

He was blind when he worked for me.

I want to continue the small talk. I'll do anything just to keep my grandfather there and engaged with me, but he looks increasingly uncomfortable.

I have to go.

Are you visiting me because of Unk? Because there's been a disturbance in the family fabric? A disturbance that reaches beyond death, that transcends time and space? Please don't go! I love having you here. There's so very much I don't understand.

He shakes his head and begins to evanesce, his image growing ever so slightly thinner and more transparent.

I try desperately to wake BA. Am I seeking to validate or confirm the experience? I am not; I know that what I'm seeing is as real as the moaning birds outside. I just want her to see Grandpa. The lines on his face, the texture of his skin, the expression in his eyes. When she won't wake up, I scoot across the bed toward him and extend my arms to give him a hug.

Don't.

But why not? You always use to hug me.

I can't.

I start to cry. To wail would be a better term for it.

I'm sorry.

I can see that he means it. I make a leap for him, ever the little boy who won't be denied, who won't be told what to do. He disappears. My arms close around nothing but a cold mist. When there is no trace of him left in the room, I go to the shower and stand under the trickle of water until the sun rises and BA does, too, finding me wracked with sobs.

———·———

Oxycontin becomes Purdue's biggest product. It's an opioid medication rife with addiction problems, though also a miracle drug for people in pain. I find myself torn between a growing criticism of the drug and the way Purdue greedily markets it to people who may not actually need it, and the fact that it is also a veritable lifesaver for those in real pain. The controversies that will later envelope the company, along with the malfeasances alleged and proven, are sad and difficult for me to accept, particularly in the context of watching my Unk's horrific passing. At one point, I have one of his doctors dangling off the floor, up against the wall of the hospital, my hands on his lapels, because he won't give my loved one the medication he needs to free him from agony at the very end of his life.

My uncle's suffering combines with my own to create an alchemical mixture, something that helps me see past the good and bad, relief and addiction, diagnosis and trauma, greed and beneficence. I see the yin and yang of things so very clearly, the blurred lines as one thing becomes the other, but not yet, not yet, do I have a formal context for all this. I'm not impressing a philosophy or belief system upon the way I see the world—I have not yet heard from a real-life Master Po—but I'm making my own *a posteriori* observations of the world and finding, as does not always happen, that they are real and consistent. Things are not black and white. They are not defined and they are not static. Thoughts and feelings, ideas, beliefs, and convictions, all are in a constant flux. Life's not a static photo but rather a movie, as rendered by the so-called *taijitu*, the drawing Western people call the yin/yang.

——————·——————

My uncle is not the only one who is suffering. My wife BA, who was once my partner but has become my dependent, is living a constrained and narrow life with no intellectual horizons available at which to gaze and no great concerns save what new pain, drugs, and mundane domestic challenge the next day will bring. I do my best in the role of caretaker and breadwinner, but I'm not having an easy time either. My primary therapy, perhaps escape is a better word, remains writing fiction. I rise early every morning before going to work and spend a few hours concocting characters and a plotline for my next novel. At the end of the workday, I come home to take care of her but as she sleeps or watches TV, I seek another outlet for my frustrations at not being able to do more to help her, at not being more patient, at generally not being a better man.

I continue with my martial arts training, always pursuing Master Po. I don't find the fictional blind master, but I do find in Westport, Connecticut, a Latino martial arts prodigy named

Calasanz Martinez. Calasanz is a direct student of Bruce Lee's kung fu brother, Moy Yat, who teaches in New York City's Chinatown. Lee and Moy Yat, in turn, are students of Ip Man, the two-time policeman and martial arts grandmaster from Foshan, a town in China's Guangdong Province. Ip Man is the teacher who turns sixteen-year-old Lee from a scrappy streetfighter into a legend, and he does it by teaching the young prodigy a southern kung fu style called Wing Chun.

Like all Chinese kung fu styles, Wing Chun enjoys a lovely origin myth, which says it originated with a nun, Ng Mui, who synthesizes a new fighting system based on the Crane and Snake systems but specifically designed for women. The new system relies on speed, precision, relaxation, and angles. A short-range fighting style, it levels the playing field between larger opponents with longer reach and smaller, female fighters. Ng Mui teaches it to a village girl, Wing Chun, to help her defeat a warlord forcing her into marriage, thereby freeing her to be with her own true love. In the story, Wing Chun, whose name means Beautiful Springtime, starts a school with her husband. The style gains cred as a practical street-fighting art and becomes popular with fighters across the globe.

If Wing Chun were a piece of classical music, it might be a baroque quintet or some other chamber selection. It has a mathematical symmetry, one that repeats and is applied to a variety of melodies, and that repetition creates stability, usefulness, a seduction of sorts, and something a musician or practitioner can practice over and over again, always looking to refine its few techniques, its handful of movements, ever closer to perfection. The style employs a training device called a *mook yan jong*, or wooden dummy. A log of red oak or other hardwood set in a frame, it features protruding wooden arms and legs that give the Wing Chun practitioner a hard, durable surface upon which to work techniques and condition the body's striking surfaces. I train for hours on this thing, learning patterns of movement through relentless repetition and increasing the density of my bones through microinjuries and calcification. In addition to being a masterful practitioner, Calasanz is a patient teacher. He recognizes that I learn slowly, have no sense of rhythm or choreography, and little flexibility. He also recognizes my innate fighting instinct, my fearlessness, my sense of my own center and how to rob the same from my opponents, and my willingness to practice basics until the cows come home.

The words kung fu (sometimes gongfu) mean hard work. Along with that work comes *ku*, the Mandarin word for the bitter taste of suffering, bitterness. There are tricks to defeat an opponent on the path of Chinese kung fu practice, but there are no shortcuts in the thousands of hours required to master the self. While Calasanz is not Po, he does help me, through all those hours spent nurturing damaged wrists, beaten knuckles, bruised elbows, and quivering legs, begin the process of transformation I've been after. He also helps me see that my body is capable of things I don't necessarily fully understand and can't necessarily reliably control.

This realization comes to light not in the training hall but outdoors, in the company of my youngest brother, Herbert, with a bow and arrow in my hand. Herbert has always been a good shooter. He was born with a fine eye, he trained himself in target practice (having set up a range in our parents' attic) and, now, a bow and arrow in their backyard. One day, while visiting my parents' suburban home, I find him shooting at a red, white, and blue target of concentric rings set into a hay bale a hundred feet or so from where he stands. I have never tried using a bow and arrow before and enjoy watching him work.

Let me try, I say, after a time. I take a couple of shots, straining against the string, struggling to hold the bow steady, not understanding exactly how to aim. Jokingly, I point to a lone leaf lying atop a roof in the great distance. It is not a great distance for a Mongolian warrior on horseback who can fell an eagle a thousand feet in the air whilst riding a galloping steppe pony, not a great distance for a Korean archer in a martial arts film whose war quiver never empties no matter how many opponents he slays, not any kind of distance for the war archers of Chinese *wuxia* epics, who rain arrows down on hapless villagers on the far side of an interposing mountain, but it is a ridiculous distance for a guy who has never shot a bow before and does not even know how to aim. The arrow flies—and it bisects the leaf. My brother screams and runs.

How is it possible that the human brain can accomplish such a thing? I'm interested in knowing the answer because, absent of any formal training in such things, I'm attempting to inject the mystical and amazing into my kung fu practice. This kind of crazy impossible happens one more time for me, again during the process of sending a projectile across an impossible distance, this time at a picnic in New Jersey. I sit with friends in chaise chairs atop a lush summer lawn. Not so very far away, pine snakes and special frogs live increasingly rare lives in the Pine Barrens. Closer, the lawn drops away, precipitously, to a deep ravine through which runs a low river; this would not be a good setting for little children.

Across the ravine, this time at a genuinely preposterous distance, is another house. Beside that house is a maple tree, its gracious branches sway as intermittent gusts of wind blast through the ravine. My host hefts the German, ten-meter Olympic air pistol I have brought along for my afternoon entertainment. He aims it at the ravine.

> *I found a target. There's another shooting enthusiast all the way over there.*

Indeed, dangling from a string tied to one of the branches, not visible as anything more than a bouncing red dot, is what my friends and I take to be a Coca-Cola can. My friend is smug about his find.

> *He put it there for shooting practice. I mean, why else would there be a can hanging from a tree if not as some kind of target.*
>
> *Foresters and biologists use cans to trap bugs sometimes.*

My friend's wife chimes in.

> *I think it's a woman's house. Everyone knows women are better shooters than men.*

We all watch the can. It remains reasonably steady for a few seconds, then suddenly swings wildly as the wind takes it. Its movements are mesmerizing, almost charming, as if it is dancing.

My friend gets a look on his face.

> *I'll bet you a million dollars you can hit that can with your little air pistol.*
>
> *Ridiculous. First, I don't have a million dollars. Besides, this little air gun uses a spring to propel a pellet. You can shoot it across the living room but not across the ravine.*
>
> *You said you could hit the head of a Q-tip with it.*
>
> *At thirty meters. That's more like a hundred.*

There's another guy at the party and he is suddenly interested in our conversation.

> I was a recon marine. I'm going to tell you that's way more than a hundred yards. The way it's moving, that shot would be impossible for a trained sniper and his spotter. Ok, maybe not completely impossible, but I'm talking mighty iffy for even with a high-powered rifle and a spotting scope all dialed in for MOA. But the way it's moving you'd need several tries and Lady Luck whispering in your ear.

My friend is even more interested now. This is how backyard barbecues sometimes go when they've gone on a few hours and everyone but me has been tippling steadily. I have to set him straight.

> Besides the marine stuff, there's the fact that the pellet just can't fly that far pushed by the little spring in my gun. It couldn't in a still room, no matter how high you aimed it. It's got no mass, it's at the mercy of gravity, and as our friend points out, at the mercy of both the updrafts from the ravine and gusting wind, too. I hate to say no to a million dollars, but to hit that can would require transcending the laws of physics.

My friend's wife is a sly one.

> I thought you were a spiritualist of some kind. Don't you believe in miracles?

My first thought is of BA.

> It's not about me. It's just not possible.

She scoffs.

Just take the shot, will you? Nobody here has a million dollars and even if we did, we're not stupid. Let's just see what happens when you try. Show us a miracle, or at least some magic.

It's a challenge I can't resist, even if just to be a good sport. I grasp the pistol with two hands and aim it at the can. I do my best to take note of anything floating in the air—a leaf, dandelion seeds, anything at all that might reveal the frequency and power of updrafts from the creek and heat down below. I count the seconds between gusts of wind. I take my time, guessing at what angle I have to aim to get the little pellet all the way downrange. It's a show and it's all preposterous nonsense but everyone stares at the tiny, distant, swinging red flash hanging from the tree.

I squeeze the trigger. The discharging pistol makes a quiet popping sound as the spring pushes the pellet downrange. A second goes by, then another, then another. The arrival of the fourth second is heralded by the triumphant *tink* of lead on aluminum as my pellet hits the can. My friend does not pay me a million dollars—that debt is still outstanding—but my definition of the word "possibly" becomes significantly broader. Driving home, I wonder whether it might not be possible for me to someday become Master Po after all, or at least *meet* him.

CHAPTER 3

ADRIFT, THEN ANCHORED

The year is 1990 and arrives when the last leaf falls from the tree and the reality of winter is more compelling than the prospect of a spring that will never come. My decision is made easier by BA's declaration that despite my sacrifice and support, there are certain habits that are more important to her than I am. I leave Purdue and head for Los Angeles, where I hope to try my hand at screenwriting. I keep a consulting arrangement with them, writing projects and such.

The terms of the dissolution of my marriage are that I give BA everything. Given that I will be able to earn again, and she won't, I do so without hesitation. What I have left are some rare United States coins, which I collected these during the Purdue years—call the move diversification—as a hedge against bank and stock market uncertainties. I have enough cash to pay for four months in my Studio City apartment. I contact my coin dealer, Janelle, whose company is in Nebraska. I ask her to start liquidating my few remaining coins. The market is in the toilet, she tells me. Hold them for a bit. She is a scintillatingly smart woman, so much so that my secretary has a standing order to put her calls through even if I'm in a board meeting. Janelle has made me good, fast money over the last eighteen months. I'm loathe to ignore her counsel, but I have no choice. Divorce has left me broke.

She wants to know how I can suddenly be in such need and is shocked to hear my news. I'm divorcing too, she says. We spend some time talking on the phone. She is a good conversationalist, more so when we are not talking about coins. She has a strong, clear voice. She tells me that Johnny Carson was from Nebraska and that Nebraskans speak the most accent-free American English there is. The fact that I can call her toll-free number and chat long distance for free doesn't hurt. I lie on the floor of my studio apartment and talk to her for hours. One day she delivers some news.

I'm coming to Los Angeles for a coin show!

Really? When?

In about six weeks.

I'm so looking forward to meeting you. I'll come to your hotel and buy you dinner. But how will I know you?

I'll know you. Your picture is on the back of your second novel, Harpoons.

That's not exactly fair! At least send me a photo.

I have no romantic ambitions for the meeting, as I have started dating someone in the movie business. Another smart woman, P advises me on my career and makes some contacts for me. I option the movie rights to *Harpoons* to actor Gene Wilder's production company. I write another novel, a thriller called *Dark Money*, about an NYPD SWAT sniper who inherits a fortune and goes around helping people. He has a giving heart but is a busybody. Once a cop always a cop, he can't help sticking his nose in people's lives. P and I spend more and more time together. One day in spring, she too has some news.

> *I just did something great for your career.*
>
> *Really?*
>
> *Really. I got you invited to Warren Beatty's birthday party.*
>
> *But I don't know Warren.*
>
> *So what? I do. This is how Hollywood works. Meeting the powerful people there will help your career, all the more so because it isn't a bash but an intimate gathering at a friend's house. We'll go together.*
>
> *Sounds great, thanks! When's the party?*

She mentions the weekend that Janelle is coming in from Nebraska. I make an intuitive, on-the-spot decision.

> *I have plans for that day.*
>
> *You WHAT?*
>
> *The coin dealer from Nebraska is coming and I am going down to meet her in Long Beach.*
>
> *You're turning down Beatty for a bumpkin!?*

Perhaps this is the moment I begin to question my life in Hollywood, which in truth has barely started. A few more projects and some success are still to come but despite having been caught up temporarily in the razzle-dazzle, deep down I know how silly it is to elevate entertainment above so many more important things, and how seriously Hollywood's self-congratulatory, narcissistic players and creators take themselves. I realize, with a sickening jolt, that I am utterly lost to Po, an imaginary figure I ironically met in the very medium I now decry.

> *I'm grateful for the invitation and sorry I can't go.*
>
> *Then we're done!*

A few days later, as I mope about what might be so important about a coin dealer I have never met—particularly when the market is in the toilet and I can't sell coins to pay my rent—my telephone rings. The call is not from Nebraska but from an old high school friend, JS, who is seriously into Buddhism.

> *I just now heard you moved to town. Heard you're a good writer, a bit of buzz going on. Selling work?*
>
> *A bit.*
>
> *Well, I'm at Disney. Have been for a while. Hey, listen, I heard you got invited to Warren Beatty's birthday party.*
>
> *Actually, I'm pretty sure I got disinvited.*
>
> *Well guess what? Since I'm the one throwing the party and it's at my house, you're invited again.*

JS and I meet for lunch on Melrose Avenue. He takes one look at me and has an opinion.

> *Dude. You want to make it in this town you have to look the part. I'm going to have to take you shopping.*

I don't have a spare nickel to spend on clothes, but I tell him that sounds great. That's when he drops the bomb.

Cool. And one other thing. When you come to the party, you have to bring a five-grand hooker.

I'm sorry, what did you just say?

You have to strut your stuff, man. She has to be the best-looking woman in the room by a mile, and your ex has to see you with her. She's already with the actor JM, by the way.

That was quick.

That's Hollywood.

Yeah, well there's no First, I don't even have the dough to pay the credit card company for the shirts I just bought, and second, I don't do hookers.

JS shrugs.

Doesn't absolutely have to be a hooker. No shortage of beauties around town. Find a girlfriend. Rent a stripper. Go down to Venice Beach and find the most jaw-dropping woman on the sand. Tell her you'll bring her to Warren Beatty's birthday party. Every girl in town wants to meet Warren Beatty. Remember, you're here to blow it up, right? You gave your ex-wife everything. You've got to make a living, man.

I leave JS's company chastened. I'm sour on Hollywood and on myself for even considering playing such a game. I move the meeting with Janelle from Saturday dinner to Sunday brunch, then I think about who I could bring to the party. I have only been in LA a short time, and I don't know anyone who fits the bill. Then I remember T, the sushi-bar waitress from San Diego. She kept in touch with me when I was in Connecticut, calling every few months to check in. I don't even know if she is still in town, still working at the restaurant, or if the number I have for her is any good. She fits the bill, though—she's flat-out gorgeous—so I give her a call. The number is still good and she sounds genuinely happy to hear from me.

Hi! How are you? Are you still married?

I tell her what is going on. She pretends to be sorry but is not very convincing.

Listen, how'd you like to go to Warren Beatty's birthday party? I'm in LA and I've got an invitation. I think you'd enjoy it and I'd love to see you.

She wails.

OMG! Of course, I'd love to go but I don't have a dress for something like that and my car won't make it to LA.

I make an on-the-spot decision. Whatever this will cost, it will be a lot cheaper than JS's initial suggestion.

I'll get you a commuter flight and we can go look for a dress when you get here.

The day of the party, I pick her up at the airport. Waiting at the gate, I worry she will no longer be what the doctor ordered. People change; I've changed. I meet her at the gate and am relieved to see she's as gorgeous as ever. We go shopping and she finds a yellow cocktail dress. We go back to my apartment. She goes to shower, and I follow her into the bathroom. She showers and I sit on the closed toilet like a gargoyle as she laughs and shakes her head.

You're such a bad boy.

I watch her do her makeup then put on the shirt I bought for the occasion, and we go to the party. JS answers the door, does a triple take looking at T, clearly pleased I appear to have followed his counsel to the letter. We go in and T makes a beeline for Warren Beatty's lap, where she sits for quite a while as I mingle with the other guests. T returns to me just in time for my ex's entrance with her new beau. She takes one look at T and disappears. Jon gives me a thumbs up. After the party, T goes home with me, not Warren Beatty. There is no magic there, sadly, as she has given her heart to some guy in San Diego. This turns out not to matter, as the next morning, I'm to meet the woman who will be my life partner and mother to my son.

I park outside the Long Beach Hyatt; I'm meeting Janelle in the lobby. This is the long-awaited, relationship-busting brunch that was meant to be a dinner. She's waiting for me, wearing a navy-blue dress and heels that show her legs. She is not only beautiful but has a penetrating gaze, a great smile, and an athletic, killer figure. When I press my compliments, she makes an admission.

I represented Nebraska in the Miss Teen USA Pageant.

Piranha in a bowl of goldfish, I think, watching the way she works the vendors, all of whom think, like 47th Street Jewish diamond dealers, that *they* are the piranhas when in fact they're fish food. I watch her make deals, batting her baby blues. I'm smitten.

I learn a thing or two about the way the coin business runs, realize that sealing coins in plastic cases with a grade assigned by an independent agency—two, actually—turns the coins into traded commodities upon which even a hedge fund is based. The problem becomes immediately apparent to me: the whole thing is a construct. There is no actual use or *need* for these coins. They are not aluminum or soybeans.

You can't build with them or eat them or feed them to your pigs. Think tulip mania in seventeenth century Holland, all hype and bound to collapse. I'm thankful I have had a good run, eager to sell the few coins I have left. I'm right about all this; the market crashes soon thereafter.

Janelle and I drive to lunch. I play music for her in the car, swapping out my favorite cassette tapes. I haven't shared a playlist with a woman since BA. We have similar tastes, although she is a bit younger and knows a few bands I don't. I advance a theory.

> *I believe we're hardwired for music between the ages of twelve and twenty-two. After that our brains just don't hear things the same way. The music we know from that developmental period of our lives will always be the music we love, regardless of what else we come to enjoy.*
>
> *I hadn't thought of it exactly that way, but I think there's something to it.*

We listen to Bob Dylan, Joan Baez, James Taylor, and Paul Simon. We listen to The Police. I try some classical. She likes it. Beethoven and Bach, nothing too daring. I venture into a little Delta Blues on her.

> *I've listened to Matt Guitar Murphy at the legendary Zoo Bar in Lincoln.*

We have sushi together. She eats raw fish with abandon, knowing the rolls she likes.

> *This might be fresher than anything we get in Lincoln. I mean it doesn't have to travel, frozen, across the country. Of course, we do have some great Indian food and some great Asian cuisine too, as the city has played host to waves of refugees.*

Janelle is anything but a bumpkin. The trouble is that she lives in Nebraska and I live in LA.

———·———

I've been so busy trying to make a living that I haven't found a school I can settle into and I've lost constancy of practice. Once again, Master Po recedes into the distance, leaving me with the nagging feeling that I need that connection to Asian wisdom and culture and practice if I am to sort out my life and find better health and more peace of mind. Halfway through 1990, I find an advertisement for aikido, a Japanese art I've always found intriguing, whirling circles and flowing skirts for men and all. The school is not too far from my modest studio apartment, so I go and watch a class. It looks nice to me, and the atmosphere is mellow. I realize I'm at Steven Seagal's school and ask the instructor some questions.

> *Wow. Does he ever come into the school?*
>
> *He travels. He does his movies. He's busy. Sometimes he shows up.*
>
> *Is he any good? I mean, the way he looks on film?*
>
> *He's big.*
>
> *I got that, but is he good? I mean, skillful? I know he married his sensei's daughter or something like that and got authentic training in Japan.*
>
> *He's big. Hard to fight a guy that big.*
>
> *Yes, yes, but is any good at the art?*
>
> *Did I mention that he's really a big guy?*

I keep looking. I find an advertisement for a Wing Chun school, the same style in which I have an instructor's sash from my time in Connecticut. I'm in the San Fernando Valley and the school is on the other side of town, far west on Venice Boulevard, a bear of a drive through notorious LA traffic, particularly at the end of the workday when all of LA is on the freeway. Still, after the visit to the aikido school, I realize it would be best to stay with a familiar style. I make the drive, and a couple of times, traffic grinds to a halt under a layer of brown air. My eyes burn and my weak lungs ache. When I finally reach my destination, I find a small place with an office at the front and a training space at the back, replete with a couple of wooden dummies and shiny butterfly knives on the wall. Grandmaster Hawkins Cheung—Bruce Lee's sparring partner and close disciple of Ip Man's—gives me a nod. He's a bug-eyed sprite of a man with comically thick glasses and he radiates an eagerness to argue, if not fight. I feel pretty much at home and I'm happy to have found a way to continue my training. I find myself hoping that maybe I will find something of Master Po in the grandmaster, so I ask if I may watch the beginner class. He agrees. I take a seat on the bench, wherefrom I notice some small stylistic differences between the version of the art I have been taught and this iteration of the same. Nothing major, though. I know I can adapt.

The beginners depart. A smaller, rougher crew trickles in, all Asians and Latinos with torn shirts, lean bodies, and tough looks. These are the senior students, some gangbangers, some biker guys with chains dripping from their jeans. They strike me as older versions of the Puerto Rican toughs I had to run from on the Lexington Avenue Subway on my way home from school, roving predatory bands that loved to chase through train cars and up and down stairs. As prey with no chance of fighting back, the best I could do was find a place to hide so they wouldn't take my stuff and beat me with a broken-off car antenna or worse.

The Wing Chun seniors assemble on their own, warm up, and begin moving. The grandmaster appears. He does not bring them to order, does not bow to them in the traditional fashion I know. Instead, he simply offers direction and pointers, though admittedly when he sees something that needs fixing his manner is emphatic, his touch hard. When the students get to work on the style's trademark wooden dummy, there is none of the sensitivity I have cultivated using the thing myself. Rather, they slam their feet, forearms, and fists into the wood with speed and force. The dummies shake in their frames. The atmosphere is different from Calasanz' school, the spirit less convivial. These are grim guys practicing a street art, apparently for their own survival. It occurs to me that I've lost this sense of existential threat since my return from South America, and that it keeps them sharp and me dull. Even so, I wouldn't care to change places with them. Having endured it, I am ever aware that violence is the lowest common denominator of human behavior.

Suddenly, the grandmaster is in the center of the room, and his hand is raised. All movement stops. All voices fall silent. He points at me, sitting on the bench.

You. Work the dummy for me.

Me?

Right now. Show what you know.

If I'm not terrified, I'm at least taken aback. I'm not ready for an exhibition, certainly not in front of these people.

I'm rusty. I got divorced. I quit my job. I moved across country. I haven't touched a wooden dummy in half a year.

No excuses! Do it!

Cheung is not my teacher and has no authority over me, but I am in his school, and it would be at least rude to refuse. Everyone must sense that I'm thinking about it, though, because the group closes in on me, a phalanx conducting me to work, no other path available. I reach out for the reassurance of the wood, finding it rock hard and warm from the gang's touches. I start moving, reminding myself of the thousands of times I have done this, of the two thousand punches I threw during my black sash test alone, the hundreds of other nights in Connecticut I threw more while snow fell and spring rains came, while summer bugs died on lightbulbs above me, while dry wind swept the parking lot clean in fall. I settle into a rhythm, pulling on the thing, slamming my forearms into it, kicking it. Nobody says a word. The sounds of impact are music.

The grandmaster suddenly yells at me.

Stop!

I drop my hands. His people move toward me. I can't imagine where this is going but it sure looks like I have got a beating coming for no reason I even imagine.

This time, when he talks, the grandmaster seems genuinely enraged.

I look at you and I see Moy Yat!

He spits a gob of phlegm onto the floor.

I'm confused. He has given me a compliment, a high one if I look anything like my own famous grandmaster, and yet he has uttered it like a curse.

Moy Yat was a bookkeeper. He knows pencils, not fists. No fighting. Only numbers. You don't know Wing Chun. You have to forget everything, learn again from the beginning. Everything you do is wrong!

There is a long silence in the hall above me, where I can barely hear the eager, martial breathing of the crowd, everyone spoiling for a chance at me. I can't avoid the lousy sense that Cheung is judging more than my kung fu. All I can do is take refuge in my respect for Moy Yat and satisfaction in being seen to move like him. I'm allowed to leave the school that night, stares like daggers at my back. I think about whether I should go back, knowing that if I don't, I will be taken for a coward.

A week later, I do go back. I train with Cheung for half a year. Once I have established that I'm not afraid of him—not afraid to hear his opinion, not afraid to change my technique for the better—I realize that he has a fixed way of seeing me that prevents him from giving me heartfelt instruction. His animus toward my former teacher is of no particular interest to me, so I leave in pursuit of a community of students with whom I can learn, and a teacher who sees me for the person I am. I try *Muay Thai*, which is Thai kickboxing. There is a teacher, Cassimore Magda, who has a school much closer to my apartment in Studio City. He is a student of the famous master Dan Inosanto, protégé of Bruce Lee. Magda tells me he thinks writers are generally lazy and full of shit. He makes me work my knees and elbows on the bag until I'm so out of breath, I vomit. I do this a few nights a week. I'm getting fitter, that's for sure. My ribs hurt and my shoulders ache and I come to know I don't want to be kicked by a real Thai boxer. I learn to cover up, to duck down, to bob and weave, to throw those elbows and knees, but there is not so much interesting culture for me behind the moves, no philosophy I can divine save move or be hit, no Master Po.

I find another teacher a few months later. Stuart Charno is down in Venice, which is another long drive, but he is worth it. Stuart is the senior student of famed New York City Chinatown kung fu master Kenny Gong. There are some stories about Gong; one time, he is on the subway reading a newspaper, and some punk pulls a knife on him and demands money. Gong takes away the knife, gives it back, and asks if he wants to try again. Another time, Gong is followed into a Chinatown alley by a Chinese street gang. They are after him with knives, chains, and guns. They set upon him near a streetlight, see his face, and one of them yells,

Run! That's Kenny Gong.

Stuart goes out to dinner with Gong one night when a group of thugs beset them. Stuart wants to help but Gong tells him to stand down, then destroys all the attackers by himself. When Stuart asks him what he did, Gong simply declares: I surround them!

Master Gong's style is Xingiquan; the name means mind form boxing. The usual legends around its origins make the truth unknowable, but there are likely connections to the Shaolin temple and the practice of the spear, which is the soul and symbol of China and its martial arts the way the katana (the famous Japanese sword) is for Japan and its fighting systems. There are animal forms in the Xingiquan, some of which appear elaborate and even flowery, but the essence of the art is tight spirals inside straight lines. The footwork is efficient and the upper body movements are conservative of both energy and distance. I find this first exposure to so-called *internal* kung fu styles fascinating. A satisfactory definition of what internal means, particularly as opposed to external, will elude me for a number of years.

Stuart is not the kind of Po-like character I have always hoped for. Even so, he is a dedicated, accomplished, and serious teacher with a great sense of humor. He and I become close friends. Shortly after I join his school, he gives up the shared space in Venice and begins teaching in the living room and backyard of his Culver City home. What I like best are the times he takes out a chalkboard and draws information about the Five Element Cycle and the applications of Xingiquan. Five Element Theory is the basis of Chinese medicine and has a deep spiritual aspect. It refers to the nature of matter, the flow of energy, the qualities of the human body, and the interactions and interface between the human being and nature. Some of the ideas are a bit complex and esoteric, but I can follow the basic idea that Xing Yi's strikes, chopping, drilling, crushing, exploding, and crossing can be connected to natural elements that have specific properties, namely metal, water, wood, fire, and earth.

Although I learn Xingiquan slowly, I find it an art well-suited to my short legs as it relies very little on kicks. I love the art's no-nonsense directness and I relish its connection to the spear; a weapon I have long been attracted to. Precursor to the gun, I figure, since the purpose is to project power over a distance, the spear, *qiang*, does not make noise, can't be used by one child to accidentally kill another, does not require ammunition and is a poor choice for a drive-by killing. All in all, I think, the spear is a lovely weapon as weapons go, though it is incredibly difficult to master—just like Xingiquan.

Compared to Wing Chun, Xingiquan seems richer, more intricate, deeper, and, in some ways, more aesthetically pleasing, though there is great elegance to Wing Chun's spare techniques and use of angles. Stuart's skills impress me greatly, as does the entire oeuvre of arts in this "internal" category. Xingiquan may have a Buddhist name like the arts practiced by Master Po at the Shaolin Temple, but, confusingly, Xingiquan (despite Muslim origins) could now be considered, at least thematically, a Daoist art. In general, Buddhist arts tend to be external and Daoist arts internal, a nuanced distinction that has something to do with where one puts one's attention while training. Daoist arts of divination and energetic cultivation are certainly shamanic and ancient, but there is some legendary basis for believing that the earliest kung fu styles were Buddhist, as they are reputed to have been taught to weak and ailing monks by Bodhidharma, the first Buddhist patriarch, when he came to Southern China from India to help them regain their health.

———————

My writing career begins to get some traction in the early 1990s. *Dark Money* and *Dark Tracks*, my novels about SWAT sniper-turned-fixer Nestor Dark, are fun to write and reasonably well-received. One day, I get a call from SR, a Hollywood literary agent. He asks me if anyone is representing the books for film and television, and I say no. He says he is pretty sure he can sell them as a series to CBS. A few days later, he picks me up in his Mercedes for my first Hollywood pitch meeting. Next thing I know, we are at CBS, which is a collection of big, squat white buildings with big, greenish glass windows. We are given badges that tell our names and who we are going to see.

Then we are in an office with Jeff Sagansky, president of CBS Entertainment, and a few of his producers. Sagansky gets right to the point.

Why should your books be turned into a TV series?

Because it's a great story that moves quickly, is written cinematically, and lends itself to episodic telling.

I think so, too.

Sagansky turns to the others in the room and in an apparently arbitrary fashion, his finger hovering in the air like a butterfly, assigns the project to a woman who sat on a nearby couch. Her face gives up nothing, something I will later remember with a combination of amazement and disgust. We move to the woman's office. She has a contract for the pilot and a couple of additional episodes on her desk. My agent reviews it. The producer's phone rings and she picks it up, covering the headset with her hand.

Would you gentlemen wait outside, please? I have to take this.

We go outside to a little waiting area with only a couple of chairs. The moment she closes the door, the agent is on his knees with his ear to the keyhole.

What the Hell are you doing?

He looks at me in surprise.

This is Hollywood. Information is king.

Yeah, well you're working for me now and I'm king. Get off the floor and stop snooping.

SR glares at me, aggrieved. A couple of minutes later, we are back in the office. We sign the contract. Back in the car, SR opens the sunroof and punches the air, laughing and clapping as we drive down Sunset Boulevard. He opens his window and yells.

We got a goddamn network series!

I'm too excited even to think of Master Po right then. A couple of days later, SR calls me.

The deal is dead.

How can it be dead? We just signed the contract.

Yeah, well, if Sagansky had given it to one of the other producers in the room, it would be alive and well and we'd be in the pink. But that woman, she's out at CBS. That phone call? It was from Hanna-Barbera. They hired her away. If you hadn't been such a big shot and had let me listen at her door, we would have known and called her on it, and we could have gotten the project moved. Now everything in her wheelhouse is in turnaround. That's Hollywood lingo for our show and everything else she was working on is dead. And you know what? She knew when she signed it that she was leaving. Knew the show wouldn't happen without her.

You mean she screwed us on purpose?

Casualty of the entertainment war. If she had refused to take on the project, she would have had to say why and she wasn't about to reveal that she was about to leave until she knew the other offer was real.

Isn't there something you can do? Call Sagansky? Get him to give it to someone else?

Tried. No go.

You want to take it somewhere else? Try another network?

Can't. That contract locks us up. We're done.

This is bad news for me on several levels, not the least of which is that I'm running out of cash. Janelle sells my remaining coins for me, but that only buys me a couple more months of rent. I call BM, the editor who bought the Nestor Dark books. He was previously at Avon Books, part of the Hearst Empire, but he has now moved up the ladder to Simon & Schuster.

I want a hardcover deal. I gotta make some scratch.

Then tell me what you've got.

A nautical thriller. Man stuff. Story of two Navy SEALs after the service, one gone bad, the other retired, they meet again over extortion and a terrorist action on the high seas.

The relationship has to drive it.

It does. Can you get me a hardcover deal?

Send me some pages and we'll see.

I call the book *The Fish Bishop*. I like the characters and have fun crafting both the good and bad guy, the former who lives on a tugboat moored on Puget Sound, the latter runs security for an oil company. I send BM an outline and the first couple of chapters.

Love it. Finish it for me.

Hardcover? I really need the dough.

You got it.

I keep sending him chapters, one after another. I don't want to take any chances that the deal won't happen. Save for the bit of money that trickles in from Purdue projects, I'm broke. I tell Janelle all about this on the phone. We talk every day, sometimes well into the night. I learn everything about her, or at least as much as she wants to tell me about her life; about her dad, who sells water tanks to farmers, her school receptionist mom, life in the howling-wind plains, tutoring football players in math so they keep their GPA and position on the team, her sister who fights with her, her alcoholic ex-husband who left her for another woman, how she went to Japan as a guest of Sony because her previous company sold so many blank Sony videocassettes, how Akio Morita, the company's founder, taught her how to use chopsticks, how she once had coffee with Carlos Santana in Sausalito but did not know who he was, how she keeps seeing Charles Bronson in the airport and that he wants to take her skiing in Aspen.

I finish *The Fish Bishop*. I'm pleased with the way it turns out. The work is a good, solid read, interesting, and different. I'm hoping for good things from BM, and after he has had time to read it, I give him a call asking for the contract and a good cash advance against royalties so I can pay my rent. He has bad news.

> *Not happening.*
>
> *What?!*
>
> *Hardcover thriller budget for the year is spent on other writers. I can't buy the book.*

I've spent the better part of a year working on this novel full time, all on BM's say-so and now he's telling me there's no deal.

> *But I sent you every chapter. If you didn't like it, wanted a change of direction, knew you couldn't buy it, why didn't you say something earlier?*
>
> *I like it very much; I just don't have the budget. Sorry.*

BM does not say it was a misunderstanding. He does not say I was wrong to think it was a done deal. He does not deny having led me on. On top of all that, he does not really sound that sorry. I think of the thousand hours or more I have spent on the book, morning, noon, and night, seven days a week, for no pay. Because of the book, I barely know anyone in town. It has been more than a full-time job for me. Now, after all that work, I have nothing to show for it.

A few days before the Fourth of July holiday, I buy myself a plane ticket to New York. I fly across the country and pitch Purdue Pharma on a project for a few dollars to tide me over, and they agree. Then I go to BM's office. I don't tell him I'm coming as I don't want him expecting me. I'm on a slow burn, the fuse red-hot and glowing. I go to an art store in town and pick up a big, portfolio-sized manila envelope—the kind of envelope that closes with a string around two paper buttons. I appear at the building's reception area and ask to see BM. The security guard stands at his podium.

Your name?

Just a delivery.

From whom?

I don't have an answer. I had not thought this far ahead. Being taken advantage of this way has enraged me, and everything comes to a boil: BA's accident, dropping out of school, the divorce, being broke, being further than ever from becoming Master Po. I make a dash for the elevator and get the doors closed just as two security guards come running. Blue blazers, rubber-soled shoes, black trousers a bit shiny from ironing.

At upstairs reception, I wave the big envelope and get buzzed through the locked glass doors. I remember where BM's office is—a corner job with a big window. I jog down the corridor until I get there. I burst in. He is at his desk, on the phone. He drops the receiver when he sees me. I approach the desk, with big strides, some look on my face that makes him run. I chase him around the office. I catch him and take him by the neck, lifting him off the ground against the wall.

> You lied to me. You totally and completely and deliberately screwed me over. Not just once, but over and over again. We talked. I sent you chapters. You could have called it off at any time, but you didn't.

He sputters. He denies nothing. He is bright red and angry, but not so angry that he wants the security guards who peel me off him to call the police. They kick me out of the building, throwing me to the street. No doubt, BM does not want me telling my side of the story all over town. No doubt he feels guilty. This is not his finest hour and nor is it mine.

I call Janelle.

> Hey there. Listen, I'm in on my way back to LA from New York. I thought I'd stop and see you. That is, if you're available.

> Wow. Well, I'm supposed to go to the Lake of the Ozarks with my parents. For the holiday fireworks and barbecue, you know.

> I'm sorry it's short notice. I've been a bit preoccupied or I would have called earlier. It's just an idea. I was hoping to see you.

She hesitates.

> Come on, then. I'll make it work.

I hang up and get to work changing the flight. The holiday makes that a bit difficult and there seems to be some weather coming in, but I get it done. LaGuardia is already socked in when I get there. The Boeing 737 to Denver pushes back anyway. I sit on the tarmac, watching the rain stream down the windows. It's 90 degrees outside, 100 percent humidity, and the plane is stifling, the air conditioning not being up to the task. Lightning flashes. Thunder booms. The captain takes to the intercom.

> *Well folks, the good news is that we are in line for takeoff. The bad news is that there are fifty planes ahead of us and the situation is the same in every airport on the Eastern Seaboard. This storm system stretches all the way from Maine to Miami.*

I have no way to contact Janelle. The only flight information I have given her is my arrival time in Denver. An hour goes by. Another one. Three more hours go by. The plane stinks of nervous sweat and frustration. Someone suggests the airline should give us all free drinks. (They know better.) Little by little, we make our way to the head takeoff position, but the line stops over and over as the storms shut down the field. Six hours after leaving the gate, we are airborne. I wonder if Janelle has blown me off by now and gone to the lake with her parents. When I land in Denver, I call her from a payphone. I tell her what's going on. She's not pleased.

> *So, are you coming or not?*
>
> *I missed my flight in Denver. I'm trying to get another one.*
>
> *Ok.*

She doesn't sound happy and I'm not happy either. I'm thinking the whole thing is a mistake, thinking I could be back in LA by now. When I finally land in Lincoln, Janelle is at the

THE MONK OF PARK AVENUE

end of the jetway, glorious in a purple sundress. I'm grungy from a whole day spent in the sweltering jets, but I get a hug anyway. We go straight to the Indian restaurant she has told me about and have a few hours to decompress and get to know each other even better. That night, at her place, we watch *Star Trek: The Next Generation* and engage in Trek Talk. She tells me what she thinks of my books and wants to know when she might see me again.

> *I may not have much money, but I have a LOT of frequent flier miles from my pharmaceutical job. I can come more often.*

She seems happy to hear this and makes an offer of her own.

> *I can also come to LA sometimes.*

———·———

Those miles run out long before they can expire. When there are none left, I tell Janelle I can't write movies in Nebraska. She tells me she is ready to leave home. I fly out, get a U-Haul for her stuff, and we drive back together. I get a bigger apartment in Westwood, and she gets a job working for a doctor's office. These are good times. There are weekend motorcycle rides in Malibu, strolls along the Venice boardwalk, window shopping in Santa Monica, a favorite Thai restaurant with hard, multicolored, triangular pillows, another place, Persian, with food so exotic we can scarcely pronounce the names of dishes. A Yale friend, Tony Eyers, sends me a card and says his best friend, Riccardo Tossani, an Australian architect of Italian descent, is living in LA. He makes the introduction, and Riccardo and I become fast friends.

Riccardo has part ownership in a small plane hangered in Santa Monica and we go flying sometimes, low, between the skyscrapers of LA at night, then once, memorably, in a sphincter clencher to Catalina Island.

My Uncle Arthur, Unk, left me a beautiful camera, a Leica M6 Rangefinder. I start using it a lot, taking pictures in and around LA—black and whites only. I find a lab and start developing and printing the work. I enjoyed photography as a student and find my return to it disciplines my creative vision in a satisfying way. I make a study of the greats, particularly the black-and-white works of Mary Ellen Mark, Henri Cartier-Bresson, and many others. I decide that despite the beauty of nature, what I really want to do is capture souls on film. I buy a medium-format camera, a Mamiya 6. Square images, high quality, lots of detail. I get more serious about photography and start selling some images. It more than pays for my hobby and becomes a source of income, albeit another modest one. Janelle seems unconcerned.

That's the way it is for artists. I knew this about you when I moved out here.

The remark startles me. I hadn't ever really thought of myself as an artist. I guess I've been too busy wanting to be Master Po.

Riccardo is offered a big promotion if he will leave town and take a job in Guam for a couple of years to oversee the sponsor's development there. I'm saddened, as he's my best friend in town. He moves away with his girlfriend. Janelle and I talk about him a lot. One Friday night, we are thinking about what to do, and Janelle has an idea.

THE MONK OF PARK AVENUE

> *We could go to that Persian place in Westwood and have*
> *that delicious rice and raisin, then maybe see a movie.*

I have a counteroffer, not as romantic but perhaps gratifying in a different way.

> *Or we could give Riccardo a call in Guam and talk to him*
> *for ten minutes. We haven't heard from him in ages. Not*
> *even a letter.*

Calling him is a random urge but we both like it. We prepare by walking Janelle's little hairless Chinese crested dog, so he won't bark while we're on the line. We make a little meal at home. When we are ready, I go to the receiver. I'm holding Riccardo's number in my hand for the first time, country code and all.

I pick up the receiver but get no dial tone; there is only dead air. I hang up, check the cord, inspect the phone's connection to the wall, and pick up the receiver again—still no dial tone, just a faint hissing noise. I jiggle the little buttons in the cradle of the beast, hoping at least that the electronic flashing I'm doing garners the attention of an operator.

> *Operator?*
>
> *Arthur?*

The voice on the other end is no telephone company employee but Riccardo himself. I don't understand how that can be, as I've been waiting for a dial tone and assistance placing this international call. I blink. I take the receiver away from my ear and put it back. The paper with Riccardo's number is on the table by the phone.

> *Riccardo?*

Arthur?

I just picked up the phone to dial you.

You just came into my mind, so I called you.

We're all stunned. How can this be a coincidence? We haven't spoken in half a year nor made any plans to do so. There is no birthday or other occasion to spur the calls. Yet some strange, otherworldly energy has led him to dial me as I dial him. At the same instant, I think of the air gun and the bow and arrow. I'm tapping the source here without intending to do so, without even knowing where to find it. I wonder if this is how Master Po lives all the time, in both the surface world and in what lies beneath, the fabric that unites all. It's a powerful experience and it sure gets me thinking.

———•———

Janelle and I move back up to Santa Barbara for a better quality of life. One weekend, I hear there are blue whales around the Santa Barbara Channel Islands. My friend Joe has a Boston Whaler, and we make a plan to go out early for a wildlife spotting adventure. We gather at sunrise; Joe has already prepared the boat. As we board, an enormous basking shark appears. A great rarity in itself, it swims between the boats in the shallow, narrow waters of the harbor like a proverbial bull in a china shop. Its fin breaks the cold, clear water, and its bulbous nose, broad head, and giant gaping maw are visible as it strains the water for plankton. Joe stares at it.

Lived here all my life, he says. Never seen one of those before. Maybe it means we'll get lucky out at the islands.

We push off into the cool, gray morning. A heavy fog bank hangs over the perfectly calm sea like a broad, gray blanket. Visibility is low and seabirds flit in and out of view, sometimes coming to rest on the surface near kelp beds that break water with brown bulbs. Several large blue sharks follow us lazily. Half an hour out of the harbor, more large dorsal fins appear, shiny black that fades to pale, scarred bodies. A dozen or more of these animals close in on the boat, making tangential passes across our wake. When they surface and blow, I know they are whales, not sharks, and wonder whether they might be Belugas, like ones I saw at the Coney Island Aquarium as a boy. The captain of a passing boat shouts across the water.

> *Those are Risso's dolphins! Almost never see them here anymore!*

We arrive at the Channel Islands. Joe steers clear of commercial whale-watching boats that are already here, heading for an area of thinner cloud cover and a shimmering patch wherein seabirds and sea lions gambol with porpoises. The porpoises surround us and ride our bow waves, shooting stars on the path ahead. We hear the pop and hiss of their breathing when they break water. Santa Rosa Island looms ahead of us. Janelle lies down on the bow alongside Joe's wife, Mary, and the two of them scream with pleasure when hard, black fins rise to their hands.

Suddenly, the dolphins are gone, and the ocean is flat. The air grows terribly quiet. A moment later, an impossibly large mountain of blue flesh breaks the surface. It rolls, then drops from sight again. The sight makes me whisper in awe.

> *Blue whale.*

It rises again, this time in the company of another. We veer toward the pair, but they keep their distance. A spout appears in the distance. We aim for it. When we get there, it erupts loudly beside us, like a scuba tank with a busted valve. A foul, fishy smell fills the air.

One of the whales passes below us. The boat rocks and the water turns white. She surfaces again, her skin reflecting the sky. Her tail is as wide as our boat is long. She moves away, a clear white patch in the water, and then circles back. This time, she comes closer, shallower, and barrel-rolls as she passes by, lazily raising a fin taller than a ranch-style house above the surface. Janelle lets out a gasp that can be heard in Montana. Joe shuts off the engine. The two commercial boats see what is going on and head full steam in our direction.

I'm sitting on the gunwale when she approaches again. This time, she is much shallower, and I can see the details of her skin. I start counting out loud as she lines up with the boat and passes directly below us, so close it feels as if there is an earthquake in the sea. Up on the flying bridge, the blood drains from Joe's face. One twitch of that massive back—never mind a flick of the tail—and we capsize in an instant. This is a hundred-foot whale. I lean over to be as close to her as possible and feel the boat shudder as she brushes us with a roll.

Her great square head appears, her pizza-sized eye looking into mine. The pupil is vast and bottomless and black, and I think I can see stars, bright pinpricks of light, in the galaxy it contains. I feel giddy, invaded but gently so, sense a probing of energy and consciousness I know I will never be able to describe. We are not the only brains on this blue marble floating in space. We are not even the smartest. After all, this whale can detect my blood pressure with her sonar, my heart rate, too, and the oxygen going in and out of my lungs. What would we do with all our fearsome brainpower, I wonder, if we did not have hands with which to manipulate and destroy? What would we say if we could communicate with each other over thousands of miles without any technology, save that which evolution provides? What do they think of us, these great beasts, as we destroy their world and butcher them like cattle? How can I convince this gentle giant that, while on the surface I may be one creature, but under the surface—my surface—I'm not part of the madness and the fray that is our society, our culture? How can I convince her that I yearn so badly for the serenity she must feel, the peace, the integration? How can I let her know I'm just trying to be Po?

The yearning to share this, and to achieve it, is so keen it brings me to tears. I'm changed by meeting the whale. My interest in Daoism, that most coherent philosophy of nature, presses a sharp edge to my brain. I want to understand exactly what lies between me and that whale, and what connects us. I deepen my studies. I continue to motorcycle the two hundred round-trip miles from Santa Barbara to LA for Xingiquan classes three times a week, hoping for answers in the occasional talks about philosophy in class. Sometimes, coming home, I have to pull over at Zuma Beach and close my eyes for a few minutes. I keep going as long as I can but there is still something missing in the training, that thing I'm still questing after. The whole five element thing is philosophy. Medicine, too, but I don't feel any change in my consciousness, just the addition of more knowledge. I'm getting older by the day, far from the boy watching Asian fantasies on big and small screens. I know I'm being stubborn, pretty sure I'm being a fool, but I still want something more.

That's when I find Master Fu Yuan Ni. He is seventy, from Taiwan, and teaches tai chi in a local hall. I've had one previous experience with tai chi in the 1970s—it was painfully slow and boring, and I vowed never to do it again. Yet here I am in front of a birdlike man who says very little, his tai chi is high up in its stance, effortless, dance-like. I'm mesmerized watching him. He is the anti-Hawkins Cheung. There's no ego to him, at least that I can see. He has no kung fu fire in his eyes, no raised, slightly wagging fingers, Bruce Lee to Chuck Norris at the Coliseum in *Return of the Dragon*: Stay down or I'll have to kill you. He's just an old guy whose wife comes to class with him and feeds him tea and snacks. Once or twice, I ask a question to understand the martial application of some movement, and he looks at me with the greatest disdain before answering.

Breaking something. Punching something.

I train with him for a year. When I try and touch him using Wing Chun or Xing Yi, I might as well be sparring with a ghost. He is so spare in his movements; I can't figure out what he's doing. And because he is so old and cool and calm, there is no heat to chase or combat sweat to smell. The leading by example is wonderful: the flow, the equanimity, they're all there, and yet it's too subtle and slow and I'm too impatient to tease out what I need from it. I'm a bit shaken by the idea that he may be *too* Po-like for me, too soft, too gentle, too *yin*. I need to sense a balance between effectiveness and sensitivity, between power and grace. Master Ni may have these things, but I'm not ready to receive them from him.

The cloud that is Master Ni is a bridge too far. I need something grittier. I find an American, DB, who trains in the Dong family tradition of Yang-style tai chi. I learn that this is the most popular style, if not the original one, and it has been simplified along the way to make it more accessible and oriented toward health. I wonder if this orientation might be just the ticket, as the martial path seemed to get my Irish up rather than cool me down. With my adrenaline running and my tactical clock ticking, it was hard to enlighten up. The trouble with DB's class—and I stick with it a while—is that there doesn't seem to be any joy in it. I wonder if this is a function of the system or a function of the man, so I go down to LA to meet his teacher. I find him full of piss and vinegar but, once again, training with him means losing two or three days of work each week to the commute.

Exasperated, I confront DB.

> Maybe I'm missing something, but I've read a few books on tai chi and nowhere do I find it written that a tai chi teacher should be a funeral director and the class should be a dirge.
>
> Maybe you'd be happier with a different teacher.

He points me in the direction of his kung fu sister, Tony DeMoulin. I ring her and make an appointment. She does only private lessons, not group classes, so I go to her house. She leads me to the patio outside, where she has a wooden practice platform emblazoned with the *taijitu*.

> Just to be clear, I'm not here to teach you form, practice, or meditation.
>
> All right. What then?
>
> The application of tai chi. It's called Pushing Hands. Some people say Sensing Hands instead. In a way, by doing rather than pretending...
>
> I don't understand.

By applying the movements so you can see how they work,
you can be sure you are doing them correctly. You will
learn balance, equilibrium, sensitivity, and a connection
to the ground called root. More, and I get the feeling this
may be important to you, you will come to understand the
underlying principles more clearly by actually putting
them into practice than you might get by just reading about
them or, worse, dreaming about them.

I suppose I have a guilty expression at that last comment because Toni smiles at me before going on.

The principles will lead you to the philosophy. If that's what
you seek, fuller and deeper understanding will come to you
through direct experience, that is through your whole body
rather than just through intellection. Living the results of
ideas will lead you to believe them more wholeheartedly.
No fantasy, just real life.

This is dynamic and interesting. Toni is passionate about the art. I can't see Master Po practicing high all the time, but if I'm straight about it, I should call him Keye Luke, the Chinese actor who played the old blind man, and who was, himself, born in 1904 in Guangzhou, China, the same place I would one day be ordained a monk. Luke was Cantonese and a man of an era where opium was still a problem for China, Britain, Hong Kong, and the rest of East Asia. Toni is a lively and enthusiastic teacher. She gets me working hard on tai chi, attacking the basics, learning the moves, and trying to cultivate the feeling of relaxation, *fan song*, that is the Holy Grail of tai chi. Relax and your energy will flow, she tells me.

That energy, *qi*, flows through channels of our body like water flows through a sprinkler system. These channels run through muscles and are often right along the paths of nerves. If we can relax enough, our muscles let go, and the channels operate in unrestricted fashion. If we get our structure right—and there is a lot about structure in tai chi—then we accomplish the dual goal of unkinking our hoses and making sure they are patent for water to flow through them unobstructed. The simple analogy makes it sound easy; it isn't. Figuring out where our posture is wrong, how we move incorrectly, and, most of all, where we are holding secret, sneaky tension—that is what Toni works on most with me. I was expecting a different kind of training but realize I'm lucky to be getting what's she's giving.

CHAPTER 4

FINDING
MASTER PO

The first time I meet my future in-laws is at a Chinese restaurant in Lincoln, Nebraska. Robert Schindler sports a gray ponytail halfway down his back, wears a ball cap, and shakes my hand with a farmer's grip. His wife, Sandra, a pretty blonde with close-cropped hair, does most of the talking, chattering on about me being from New York and my father being a famous doctor. The waitress brings menus. Bob touches her on the arm.

Darlin', please bring me five Scotches. In shot glasses.

Five?

Five.

In the wake of this, the rest of us pretend to be busy with the menus. The waitress brings the Scotches and lines them up in front of Bob like pawns on a chess board. Staring at me, he takes the first one, downs it in a gulp, and exhales

THE MONK OF PARK AVENUE

loudly. A cloud of Scotch wafts across the table. Second one. Gulp. Exhale. Third one. Fourth one. Fifth one. At the end, he leans in.

So what's it like to be a Jew?

My mother-in-law, Sandra, reads my expression. She reads the one on her daughter's face, too.

The way you people emphasize education. We like that.

Janelle excuses this later. She tells me Bob is the opposite of an anti-Semite, that in fact he suspects there is Jewish blood in his family line. After all, she says, his name is the same as the name of the famous Pole who saved all those Jews during the war, the one they made the movie about.

You know Schindler was a gentile Pole, right? I mean, not Jewish.

Well, we have other reasons. There aren't many Jewish people in Lincoln. One owns a car dealership and is very rich. Jews are rare here. They fascinate my father. They fascinate me. You fascinate me.

I hope for some reason other than my genetics and heritage.

She gives me her spectacular smile, ever so slightly lascivious.

Oh yes! Many other reasons!

———•———

In 1992 I decide to revisit Paraguay. I'm really in search of how I feel being there. I want to know what I've accomplished in twenty years and what new perspectives I can bring looking at that thorny jungle through my camera. My old friends and I enjoy a grand reunion, and while I enjoy photographing the marginalized lives of the indigenous Guarani people along the soft borders of Asunción, I yearn to see the harsh but beautiful landscape of the Chaco. It's summer, not winter, and the landscape is completely different—a subtropical wonderland rather than a dusty hell. I hire a Cessna similar to the one that rescued me, but with two seats and no mail bag. My destination is the research station where RMW and the others abused me. I want to smell Palo Santo trees again.

We drone west from the capital at five thousand feet. My eyes are trained on the horizon in anticipation of the biodiversity I know is there: the bountiful bird species, jaguars, and snakes. Despite what transpired there, I have such clear and fond memories of the landscape that the place has become synonymous with nature for me, the quintessence of all that is wild and special and real in the world. The farther we get from the city, the more surprised I'm by the dust clouds rising before us and the pervasive brown of the landscape. I query the pilot.

Where is the Chaco? Shouldn't we see it by now?

You're looking at it.

That is when I see the cattle. There are so many of them that I have not noticed them at first. By this, I mean, they cover the ground so completely that I think they *are* the ground. East and west, north and south, everywhere there is nothing but dust and cows. Gone are the trees and the lakes and ponds and the serpentine watercourses I remember. Gone is anything growing higher than my knee.

What happened here? It looks like global thermonuclear war.

Cheap hamburgers for America happened. Wendy's. McDonalds. Burger King.

The scale of what I see defies imagination. From horizon to horizon—and the horizon is far more distant in a plane—the entire ecosystem, a whole part of Planet Earth, millions of years in the making, has been entirely erased in just two short decades. Irreversibly transformed. Irredeemably destroyed.

What have we done?

The pilot just shakes his head. The evidence of manmade catastrophe is so undeniable and overwhelming that I feel a terrible pit in my stomach. My eyes fill with tears. Oh no, I say. No, no, no. This is the moment it hits me. This is the moment I realize that there is no more important crisis in the world than this, no more important subject for discussion and rectification. This is when I begin to wonder what Master Po would say if he were beside me and what Asian philosophy might have to teach me—not only about how to achieve and maintain my emotional equilibrium, but how to see nature differently than mainstream Western culture does, and how to see our own place in nature differently from the disastrously deluded role presented by the faiths of Abraham and his descendants.

This is the element, the experience, that moves me from *questioning* Western society, values, religion, and culture to outrightly *rejecting it*. Master Po is a fictional character and his presence in my imagination seems all the sillier the older I get, but I remain convinced that I will someday find his flesh-and-blood incarnation. As it turns out, when I do, he doesn't look at all like what I expected and I don't meet him in the mountains of China, either, but in crowded, boisterous South Florida.

———.———

Four years later, in 1994, Janelle and I marry overlooking the Pacific Ocean, on the restaurant veranda at Post Ranch Inn on the Big Sur Coast. Eagles swoop and dive past us as a cliff-rescue ambulance driver who doubles as a New Age minister on weekends presides in a purple robe. We have lemon chiffon cake and are surrounded by friends, many of whom have come in from the East Coast. Before the festivities, I wander down to the bar in my double-breasted dark green wedding suit. I find Bob Schindler there. Even though noon has yet to arrive, he is longingly caressing a bottle of Johnny Walker Black Label. The shocking thing is that he is wearing the exact same suit I am. We stare at each other. I break first.

> *Come on! Where's you get it?*
> *Men's store in Omaha. You?*
> *Beverly Hills.*

He smiles.

> *Bet you paid more.*
> *Bet I did. And this is the least expensive thing about this day.*

His smile broadens into a grin. It's a good one—charming, that of a salesman's.

> *You got that right.*

The bartender opens the whiskey for us. We start in on the bottle. Outside, there is the occasional wail of a seagull.

Sometimes, right when the waves pull back from the rocky beach far below, in that moment of eerie silence, we can hear a seal bark. Even after a couple of pretty full glasses of Johnny, I can make out the difference between the heads of sea otters and the floating balls of *Macrocystis* kelp, the part of the plant that keeps it buoyed at the surface. My heart's adversarial relationship with alcohol prevents me from being a five-shot-a-day guy (indeed generally speaking I barely tolerate a single drink) but nerves keep me relatively sober all the way down the bottle.

Janelle and I spend our wedding night in a treehouse. The next morning, we set off on my old BMW motorbike for a two-wheeled honeymoon ride up the coast to Mendocino. When we return home to Santa Barbara, we do so with the feeling that maybe we are starting to outgrow the town. A few months later, Janelle tells me she has some news.

I want to be in the cigar business.

I blink.

What?

I see a trend coming. You know I'm like Faith Popcorn. I can see the future of business. I notice things.

I know my wife is literally a genius, IQ scores and all, but it had never occurred to me to think of her as someone who could spot social trends and use them to excel in business.

Ok, but cigars?

No pun intended, they're going to be hot. Plus, I've always loved their smell and that the good ones are handcrafted, a real luxury item that almost anyone can afford, at least sometimes.

Go for it.

She does, and a few weeks later, the world's largest manufacturer of premium cigars flies her out to Florida for an interview. Not long after that, they offer her an executive position. She's concerned I won't leave California.

Will you go? Will you move to Florida?

Film, I have learned the hard way, is a director's medium. I have never been comfortable being a director's do-boy the way writers are. There is an old joke about the starlet who comes to Hollywood and is so dumb, she sleeps with the writer. I want my own creative visions to be my work, not a collaboration or someone else's interpretation of my work. Much of what I write, just like much of what I photograph, is part of my own spiritual and artistic quest. I realize I don't play too well with others, and I don't have much respect for the entertainment industry. Besides that, Janelle moved to California for me. It's my turn.

All right. Let's give it a try for a year or so and see how it goes. I'll go back to focusing on books that I can write for the sake of creating something beautiful and telling a great story.

Still relative newlyweds, Janelle and I caravan across the country for the second time in six years, this time in a rented minivan. Janelle's new employers are so eager to have her they pay to move even the modest collection of vintage BMW motorcycles I've put together over the years. We drive instead of fly because we have our pets to bring, which include a Mexican hairless dog and a Chinese crested dog.

Also, in the back of the van, swimming in their own fragrant and liquid feces within the first half hour of the drive, are three giant tortoises. One is a fifty-pound female Aldabra Island Giant I bought in 1982 when it was the size of a tennis ball. The other two are five-pound Galapagos giant tortoises, a female and a male, which we traded for a fancy tea set given to us as a wedding present by wealthy friends of my parents.

We arrive in Florida, and Janelle is off and running with her job. I take a bit longer to settle in. Since the break with BM over *The Fish Bishop*, as well as my ditching my Hollywood manager and bowing out of a project I was doing for uber-director James Cameron's development executive, I'm in a bit of a dry spell with writing. I have left my tai chi teachers, too, so the best I can do is get a membership at LA Fitness and teach a weekly class on Chinese internal arts in lieu of family dues. One day, a guy comes into class and hands me a slip of paper that might be part of a paper towel, as it has some texture.

Call this guy. He's just in from China and his kung fu is really good. I'm sure you'll want to meet him.

I thank him and take the paper but forget all about it. A week or two later, I find it crusted and balled up in my pocket. I manage to unfurl it and read the number. I dial it. Just like that, no forethought, no foreshadowing of life about to take a left turn, either.

What a lot of people don't realize about left turns is that they don't just happen. Inevitably—universally even—there is a lot more going into any left turn than is evident at the moment, the moment the tires squeal and gravity tugs at our jowls. At some point, there had to be a reason to build a road. At some point, the road is built and the turn is incorporated, because there is a reason for that—to guide travelers toward, away from, or around something. At some point, we have to elect to take that particular route, to use that road instead of another one—the winding one instead of the superhighway in my case, because I have always been a blue highways kind of guy. Then, of course, there is the turning. The picking of the line through a curve, the skillful application of the brakes before the actual change of direction, the lifting of the eyes to a new horizon—perhaps clouds where there was previously blue sky, perhaps the other way around. The way most of us live, all we really do is look at that next horizon. We rarely pay attention to the road itself, which is why some of us enter turns too fast, skid off the road to crash and burn, or, perhaps almost as bad, miss the turn entirely and end up in some kind of existential oblivion.

I make the call. The Chinese guy's English is not perfect but better than my Mandarin. We arrange a meeting at a café down in Hollywood, forty-five minutes from my house. I get there a little early, roll of the morning traffic dice, and am there when the guy walks in. Master Yan is 125 pounds, with hair like a porcupine and a freckle on the end of his nose. He's ten years my junior, and his name means High Flying Bird in Chinese. We exchange pleasantries. He is very serious about eating his breakfast and the silences are a bit awkward for me, so I go on a roll.

I've won some tournaments.

He nods.

I've been in some fights. Done pretty well.

He grunts.

I've got a few black belts.

He concentrates on his eggs.

We come to the end of our meal, and he surprises me with a proposition.

Wanna move around a little bit?

Sure!

We pay the tab and go for the door. Right then the sky opens up and raindrops the size of quarters attack the street. We huddle under the awning, a yard from the tables inside. He looks around at the rain and then points at the ground.

Right here?

All right.

We each put out a hand, formally, as if in a kung fu movie. If we had robes, we would tuck them into our belts to keep them out of the way, so we could jump up onto rooftops and sail over the crown of the city like cranes. The back of my right wrist touches the back of his right wrist, and all of sudden, I'm sitting down. I leap up and rub my coccyx.

Sorry. This wet pavement is so slippery.

He smiles. We touch again. Down I go. As far as I can tell, he has not done anything. I don't see or feel him move but somehow, I'm on the ground again. This time, I come up with another excuse.

It's these shoes. They're smooth on the bottom. Like road-racing slicks. You know, tires on a racing car. Not meant for the rain.

He smiles one more time and once more, we touch. Down I go. I get up more slowly this time. I look at him with suspicion. Something uncomfortable is growing in my mind.

All that stuff I said about what I've won and done? Forget it. Whatever it is you know; I obviously need to learn it.

He shakes his head.

Never mind. I'm busy.

With those words and not a word more, he buttons his jacket and heads off into the storm.

On my drive home, I'm filled with such self-loathing I worry my heart will stop. I hammer on the wheel of my pickup truck. *I'm such an asshole. I should have listened more and talked less.* I shout imprecations at myself over the drum of the rainstorm, and I keep shouting them halfway home. Gradually, I realize that the reason I'm so mad is that I somehow sense—even though I know absolutely nothing about him—that the person I just met is the one I've been waiting for since I first read *Laozi* and *Zhuangzi* and the masters of Zen in my mother's library in Manhattan. He is, dare I say it, my real-life Master Po.

I don't know how I know this. Perhaps I sense some esoteric energy, perhaps I merely appreciate his skill. In whatever way I know it, know it I do, and the certainty makes me loathe myself all the more. I continue down the road in a state of excruciating angst. Squinting through the wipers and the rain, I try to keep my truck on the road until something happens. This may be the best thing about me: I can turn self-loathing into a steely resolve to change. I do this. I judge myself harshly, I learn from my mistakes, and I hold myself to a high standard, even though I usually fall short. The one thing

I conclude, just as I pull into my driveway, is that whatever it takes, I'm going to fix this. Master Yan is going to teach me, and I'm going to learn from him.

That same night, the student who gave me Master Yan's phone number shows up in class. The moment I see him, I run over and grab him by the lapels. Since assaulting my literary agent in New York, this seems to have become my MO.

> *What the Hell are you doing? Get off me!*
>
> *I need an address!*
>
> *What are you talking about?*
>
> *The Chinese guy you introduced me to. I need to know where he lives.*
>
> *I have no idea where he lives!*

I let him go.

> *I'm sorry. I'm going through something. No excuse, I know. I hope you can forgive me. I would sure appreciate it if you could get an address.*

In response, he storms out to use the gym phone, comes back in, and throws a piece of paper at me. I never see him again.

The next morning, I'm up at five o'clock. I shower, dress, and make a sandwich. I put the sandwich in a box and mix some lemonade in a jug. I take a paperback and a sunhat, heading out the door. Janelle wants to know where on Earth I'm going. There's something I have to do, I tell her. I don't know how long it will take.

> *What's going on? Do you have a woman?*
>
> *I have you.*

I drive down to Hollywood again. Right at six o'clock, I park my car near Master Yan's house and establish myself on the curb outside. Two hours later, he emerges. He sees me and walks past, saying only a single word:

You.

Despite his evident disgust, I wait for him to return. I don't know his schedule, don't know whether he will be back in twenty minutes or at the end of the day. I'm so afraid to lose sight of his door, I don't turn away even for a moment. The heat is sweltering, and it rains in the afternoon, but I stay put. Once I relieve myself behind a ficus, my eyes still on his door. At five o'clock, he is back. He sees me again, walks right past me, goes into his apartment, and slams the door.

I'm back the next day. All day. He comes, he goes. He doesn't look at me or offer a single word. I'm there the day after that. All day. Again, nothing. I make a move toward him, he vanishes like a ghost, just like Master Ni. Days go by. The first week. Nothing. The second week, Janelle is ready to commit me to an institution. If she were a less marvelous person, she wouldn't accept that this is just something I have to do. That second week, it rains a lot. Not constantly, but at least every day. I wear a slicker and carry an umbrella, too. My book is ruined. My pants get wet. My slick-bottom kung fu shoes grow soggy and stink. Friday, Master Yan confronts me.

You're stalking me. Go away or I'll call the police.

I've been waiting all my life for you. I have to learn what you know. Please. I'll do anything.

He waves me away, gets in his car, and drives off. One more week goes by. On the twentieth morning, he comes out and sees me on his curb, huddled in the drizzle.

You're very persistent.

I can be that way when something is important to me, and this is. You are. I'm sorry for talking more than listening. I'm an idiot and I made an idiot's mistake. Please teach me.

He looks at me for a long time.

I'll see you in the park tomorrow morning at nine o'clock. Don't be late.

Instead of stubbornness or self-loathing, this time while I drive home I can barely contain myself. I'm just so grateful and excited.

On the way to the park, I leave enough time to fix two flat tires and not be late. I get there an hour early. Master Yan shows up with some tea and a Chinese newspaper. He sits at a table and makes himself comfortable.

Today, we stand.

I don't trust myself to speak. No comments, no questions. He positions me in a certain way, feet shoulder width apart, arms up like I'm embracing a tree.

Put the tip of your tongue on the roof of your mouth behind your front teeth. This completes the energy circuit in your body, which runs up the middle of your back and down the front of your midline. Now close your eyes and stand like this for an hour. Whatever you do, don't move.

After a few minutes, my scalene muscles start to burn. Since my eyes are closed, I can't see him, but somehow I know he's watching. He offers a single word.

Relax.

This is hard to do when the sides of my neck feel like they have been shot with flaming arrows. My muscles are not used to holding up my arms this way, either, so a few minutes later, my deltoids feel like they have been stabbed. The pain there helps me ignore the pain in my legs, but those hamstrings and quads are the largest muscles in the body and after a time, their screams can't be denied. My quads ache most but both legs hurt everywhere.

After all that I have been through trying to get this lesson, I would rather have spinal fusion than give in to the pain. The only way my arms are going down is if they spontaneously fall off my body. I breathe. I try to think happy thoughts. I turn my attention to the birds. I try to smell squirrel pheromones in trees. I try to feel the energy Master Yan tells me is circulating through my body. I do all kinds of things, but the one thing I can't do, the one thing I won't do, is move. At last, the hour is over and I'm awash in relief. Master Yan has only one comment.

How about that's all for today?

I pay him for the lesson. He nods, puts away his tea, folds his newspaper, and walks off to his car. Over his shoulder he says what I really want to hear.

Day after tomorrow, same thing.

———·———

A few years into my training with Master Yan, I visit Hong Kong. It's 1999 and the British are two years gone. I have traveled light enough not to check any baggage. The biggest single thing I have is a trio of hardcover books in my knapsack. They are the complete translation of Louis

Cha's *The Deer and the Cauldron*. These books, this entire category of literature, has me looking at my writing career in a new light. They are *wuxia* novels, martial arts fiction, the literary foundation of kung fu movies produced by the Shaw Brothers, which are those crazy, campy, chop-socky films I have enjoyed for years (the ones so badly dubbed that everyone makes fun of them but marvels at the choreography and the costumes). Like those movies, these are popular works—hugely popular in fact. Like some other famous examples of great literature masquerading as pulp fiction—Charles Dickens comes to mind—his are appreciated for what they are, perhaps because Cha, a Hong Kong newspaper tycoon, is a well-known public figure.

To set up what remains one of the most perfect afternoons of my life, I have the second volume in my knapsack as I enter Hong Kong's world-famous Peninsula Hotel. I make a beeline for the lobby restaurant, get a table and review the menu, which includes some of the best *dim sum* anywhere. I make my order, choose a fine oolong tea to help me digest the food, and pull my book out of my bag. For the next five hours, I'm transported to an ancient China where the weird, wild, and mystical still obtain, where both men and women have the time and opportunity and passion to engage the pursuit of arcane skills that earn them a living as warriors and bodyguards, but also to build minds like Master Po's. In short, I'm in Heaven.

Master Yan has allowed me to see how a traditional Daoist training program intermingles and coheres history, philosophy, art, and movement together under one umbrella, the better to achieve insight, compassion, equilibrium, power, and poise. Even the arcane texts I read as a child begin to make sense. After decades of dreaming, I not only see the far shore, but I have a boat to help me reach it. More, I see a way to meld my literary creativity with my passion for exotic esoterica. I see a way I can be both the spiritual person I have always wanted to be and the artist who has a message worth sharing. I have traveled all the way to Hong Kong to breathe the world I want to render and register details for my next novel, which will blend elements of *wuxia* with my own Western, literary sensibility.

I conceive a rafter of characters on this trip. One is a neurosurgeon possessed by the spirit of his teacher who goes out in Miami at night as a vigilante on a motorcycle, taking lives with his sword—he really knows how to cut—but only lives that need taking. Others are a brother and sister alive for thousands of years courtesy of the energy exercises *qigong* they learned from their father in Neolithic proto-China. I conjure the lives these people live, the garden atop Victoria Peak in which the ancient sister tends her orchids and shrugs off the bite of a deadly viper. Likewise, I envision the brother, who cannot stop loving the people he will inevitably lose. I conceive situations, settings, paradoxes, opportunities, and conundrums enough to drive the plotlines of years' worth of novels and screenplays. When I have had my fill of Hong Kong, I return to my teacher and my training.

When I'm not with Master Yan or writing books, I teach tai chi at a wellness center in a Fort Lauderdale hospital. The place is ahead of its time, using music, massage, aromatherapy, counseling, acupuncture, and movement to bring souls into congruence with who they should be to shed illness, to traverse the world with delicate steps, never so much a toenail awry. The financial model is not viable long-term, and everyone knows it, but we enjoy it for as long as we can. As what will obviously be the last staff Christmas party approaches, the director motions me into her office.

Will you attend the bash?

I wouldn't miss it.

Good, because there's this guy who's been hanging around and I want you to meet him.

What kind of guy?

He says he represents a company that manages places like our center, knows how to make them profitable, a turnkey thing, a program we buy into and he takes over everything.

I go to the party. There are bad dips, stale chips, soda cans, and a plastic tree. There are people hovering around who would never mesh but for their shared sense of purpose. The director brings the guy she talked about over to meet me, but before she does, she wants me to have a look at his handbook and the document his company has prepared for the center. I start leafing through the three-ring binder, and quickly realize that it bears the logo of the martial arts school that wanted to train me to be a mob soldier. I get a cold feeling, surprised of course, but also some kind of internal nod of expectation—that I knew the universe could and did serve up this kind of twist all the time, and that I should not be taken off guard by such things.

I'm a bit more surprised by the face of the man who goes with the book. I recognize him as one of the "scorpions" who stood beside the "bullfrog master" all those years before. He knows me as quickly as I know him, and we nod to each other, circle the Fritos, make no small talk, offer each other nothing. Later, the party thins out, and we find each other outside the hospital building in the parking lot. What I remember about this particular scorpion is that he has the rep for being a smooth streetfighter, which in the martial arts world means he is a treacherous, duplicitous realist with no code or ethics. In short, he is the kind of guy who will do whatever it takes to win. I'm a bit scared of him. My mouth is pretty dry. He is not particularly tall, standing on the curb while I'm on the asphalt, taking any and every advantage, including the purely psychological, to intimidate before combat. I step up onto the curb until we are on equal footing.

> *You can't come here.*
>
> *No? Are you sure?*
>
> *Absolutely.*
>
> *But we're going legit, and we want a legit business.*
>
> *Find another opportunity. There are plenty of other places to go.*
>
> *I like this one.*
>
> *Even so.*

There might be a tinge of surprise in his expression. It might also be derision. I don't know him well enough to be sure.

> *You understand they're going under. Going out. Closing the doors.*

I nod.

> *Better that than get involved with you people.*

His eyes run me up and down, ice cold as he calculates the odds.

You understand who you're talking to.

I do. And since you're keen to go legit, don't you think it would make good business sense to follow the path of least resistance and go somewhere else rather than insisting on coming here?

His breathing picks up. We stand like that for a moment. Nose to nose, fists balled, rocking on our feet. At last, he nods.

Be seeing you.

He backs away and so do I. For the second time in fifteen years, I sleep with a gun under my pillow expecting I will have to use it. A few days later, I find out he has withdrawn his offer to manage the center. A year or so after that, I find out he bankrolls what is to become a famous healing spa up in Palm Beach. When I do, I think about what I would have done if he had struck first out there in the parking lot. Gone down, I suppose. He was a better fighter than I was. The thing is, most of us don't know what we will do until we are actually in a situation. We see these things in a movie, read them in a book, and tell ourselves lies. Most of us would just freeze or piss our pants. I learned some things about myself in Paraguay and Ecuador, and holding that knowledge made me more powerful than I otherwise would have been. Maybe the scorpion sensed that somehow.

Certainly, he must have sensed Master Yan's presence in my life, though I never mention my teacher at all. Master Yan's students choose him just as much as he chooses them. He counts among them—the serious ones, that is—a former marine sniper turned bomb squad detective, a mafia chieftain, an anesthesiologist, a wedding photographer, a real estate agent, a police chief, a Princeton physics professor, a Texas academic mathematician, and a handful more. As I learn more about him, I discover that his family were once rulers of the Kingdom of Yan, an area located along the seacoast to the north of Beijing and a distinct kingdom starting in 323 BCE. In a culture that venerates ancestors and is proud of its history, Master Yan's family lineage means the world, at least among educated people who have not been stripped of their past by the modern Chinese regime. In short, his is a famous family name.

That Kingdom of Yan? It was one of the last seven states to exist before being conquered in 221 BCE by the oppressor, Qin Shi Huangdi, a murderous tyrant who set the tone for later ruthless rulers by calling conquering "unification," slaughtering those opposed to him, and imposing all ways of life upon his victims, from the width of wagon wheels to language and currency. In his desire to expunge everything that had come before him, to pretend he was the first ruler and originator of all culture, he exterminated all intellectuals, burned all scrolls, and took control of all infrastructure. Mao Zedong followed his lead when he brought his brand of communism to China, and Xi Jinping has done the same, moving ever further from Karl Marx's utopian vison of economics and society and ever closer to total and irresistible tyranny.

In finding Master Yan, I have found a veritable Leonardo da Vinci of Daoism—not just Chen family tai chi and numerous other martial arts, but of Chinese history and philosophy, literature, and painting. Chinese martial arts. I figure that his august lineage must have opened doors for him in getting the training he did, although his obvious genius as both an athlete and an intellectual surely has not hurt. His trajectory learning from the greatest living tai chi masters started when he was seventeen years old, in poor health from rheumatic fever. After that, his training was proverbial, like something from a *wuxia* novel. Recognizing his gifts, the grandmaster apprenticed him to a series of tai chi legends, in each case assuring that, as he slept on couches and cleaned up houses, he learned different specific skills, including sword sparring, open-hand fighting, traditional weaponry, Daoist philosophy, and *qigong*.

Master Yan has an omnivorous appetite for facts and ideas; he has a flawless, computer-like memory and a penchant for fluid dynamics and aeronautical engineering. He brings all this to bear on tai chi mechanics, rectifying the way I stand, move forward, step sideways, shift my weight from leg to leg, and retreat. One day, I come early to my lesson with him (at the school the *mafioso* opened for him on Hollywood Boulevard) and overhear another student griping about me.

> How come that guy, Arthur, gets to learn so much. How come you show him stuff you don't show others?

Master Yan is typically implacable in the face of this inappropriate outburst.

> He practices a lot.

> I practice just as much. I'm in all the same classes he is. I take as many private lessons as he does.

> He teaches a great deal. In his classes, he repeats all the basics over and over.

> But I practice the basics, too!

I'm not supposed to be hearing any of this. I'm in the little antechamber to the school, near the back door, the spot where students leave their shoes. Master Yan continues to patiently rebuff his student's complaints.

> *Maybe I can make this clearer. When I go to his house, he washes dishes with tai chi movements. When he puts them away in the cupboard, he shifts his weight with tai chi movements. When he drives his car, his hand does tai chi spirals on the gearshift. Even his foot spirals on the pedal. If you want to learn the art, this is what you have to do. The movements enter your body like a virus; the ideas enter your mind like a virus.*

Hearing this, I decide to make myself known. I open the outside door again and close it loudly. At length the other student leaves and I enter the practice hall. On one wall, punching and kicking bags are suspended. In a corner, a bunch of traditional Chinese battlefield weapons are clustered. On another wall are ten plastic frames in a line. Each frame details the requirements of a level of achievement in traditional Chen-style tai chi, the original and ancestral form of the art created by Chen Wang Ting, a Ming dynasty general and member of the ninth generation of the Chen family. The general drew upon Daoist teachings from an unknown monk, the martial traditions of his wife's family, and traditional Chinese medicine, this last as to be able to break something in those old days required that you also know how to fix it. There were no ambulances or hospitals. The power of life and death, health and disease, all rested upon village sages and elders.

The first level detailed on the plaque on the wall is the beginner's level. It entails rectifying the body, alignment, relaxation, sussing out the places where we are inflexible or immobile or stuck energetically and beginning to attend to them. The second level requires some memorization of a sequence of movements. The third level is tai chi expert. Master Yan tells me that more than 99 percent of people who study tai chi *seriously* finish their lives there. To complete this level is an achievement of significance. A fourth level practitioner is a tai chi professional and requires mastery of certain traditional Chinese weapons of war. A fifth level practitioner is a tai chi master. Levels five through ten represent not only great martial prowess but esoteric powers and talents as well.

Upon the conclusion of my private class, Master Yan casually tells me to go buy a *guan gong dao*, a seven-foot pole with a spear on one end and a blade on the other, similar to what Europeans call a halberd. Looking at the framed requirements on the wall, I realize this is his indirect way of telling me that I have now entered level four. I'm so incredibly excited by this that I rush home and find a vendor for the giant thing. I make some calls and find a place in the Midwest that carries one imported from China. Excited as a six-year-old at Christmas, I pay more to have it shipped to me quickly than I pay for the sword itself. A few days later, I return to Master Yan's school, halberd in hand, exultant.

I got it!

Good. We will start learning it today.

Before we do, could you show me the sequence of movements I'm going to learn? The only place I've ever seen one of these is on a kung fu movie.

The form is very long and difficult. We should just start at the beginning.

Maybe just show me a few movements? You've seen people do it, but I never have.

All right, he says. I'll show you the first forty. Remember,
this is used to strengthen the hips, the dantian, and teach
the brain to deal with intricate footwork.

Even when he is limiting himself to render things more accessible and reproducible, watching Master Yan move is always a treat. He is so much better than the movie performers, because not only does he move as gracefully and beautifully as they do, he also moves with genuine power and without cinematic enhancement. I expect to be intimidated but in fact what I see inspires me. To say he has very intricate footwork is an understatement. There is leaping and jumping, twisting and turning, rapid switches of the lead foot, as well as sinking into low, twisted stances to sit on one heel and then explode upward. As promised, the hips are mightily employed. And that's just the lower body. Slashing, chopping, blocking, and slicing with the massive blade are another matter, as all of these are controlled by frequent turns of the waist, intricate rotation of the wrists, and repositioning of the elbows and shoulders. All in all, the performance is both dazzling and intimidating. When he is finished, he suddenly thrusts the giant sword into my hand.

Now you.

Here is the thing about what happens next. I'm not really present. I'm not thinking about how to do what I just saw, not running the usual tape about my own clumsiness—Master Yan often declares, disgusted, that I move like an elephant when I should be leaping lightly from one lily pad to another like a pond frog—or how I take forever to learn choreography. Instead, I just pick up the weapon and proceed to repeat the movements I just saw. When I finish, Master Yan stares at me with something akin to slack-jawed amazement. I have never seen this expression on his face before. Generally, he is impatiently waiting for me to do something he has just shown me and trying, unsuccessfully, to hide his conviction that I'm a cretin.

I didn't know you could do that.

I didn't know I could do that either.

Hmm. Arthur Rosenfeld, tai chi genius.

Upon hearing these words, I do a spontaneous rooster walk around the room. I can't help myself. Master Yan is generally quite sparing with any kind of compliment, so naturally I'm in shock. After all, one of the world's greatest practitioners has just called me a tai chi genius. He is not particularly amused.

Do it again.

I stop my idiotic prancing and place the weapon blade up, edge forward, the spear point on the ground by my right baby toe in the starting position. That, sadly, is as far as I get. I'm completely frozen. A block of ice. A slab of granite preserving eons of Earth's history in its dark and striated immobility. Master Yan waits. I think. I try. He waits some more. Finally, when I realize I'm not going to get past it, I lay down the sword.

Sorry. I've got nothing.

Hearing this, seeing it, Master Yan appears vindicated in the opinion he held of me before the anomaly that just appeared and vanished. He snorts.

Tai chi idiot.

And there I go. High as a kite, a genius, then back down to the doldrums; an idiot slogging away. He doesn't exactly take pity on me.

You know what happened, right?

I forgot the routine.

He shakes his head and then delivers a comment that will become a theme in my training for a quarter of a century.

No. Well, yes, but that's not really what happened. What really happened is that your mind got in the way. You have to learn to get out of your own way. You have to get out of your own way in everything. In your writing. In your practice. In your living. You try too hard. You think too much. Most of the work we have to do is you figuring out how not to do that.

So that's it. That's the secret of Master Po's life. Master Po, I'm learning from his real-life counterpart, is not in his own way. Over the decades to come, I will learn that Master Yan has his foibles, that he is in his own way too sometimes, but he is a real person and Master Po is not, and he is in his way less often than most of us. In Western terms—a twist on Jung and Freud—self-awareness is good, but self-preoccupation is not. Said differently, to accord with nature and live a fully realized life we must come to know our true nature and, once we have done so, obey it without struggle or complaint.

This can be as a process as painful as a complex dental extraction without anesthesia. The offending tooth (the ego) may be grievously intertwined with other teeth (ideas, people) and, perhaps, even anchored, in some pathological way, to the underlying bone (beliefs, culture, family lore). It also leaves out the fact that the tooth under consideration is in danger of fragmenting into countless little shards of enamel and pulp, and by doing so, become utterly impossible to pull. Identifying and coming to terms with who I really am means repairing the damage done in childhood and stripping whatever learned behaviors, no matter how adaptive they may seem, that obfuscate the truth about my own character, identity, proclivities, weaknesses, and strengths. I must gather myself and I must cohere. I must, in short, become a Daoist.

There comes a point in every artist's life where he or she must abandon all hope. The trope of the starving, frustrated, and stymied writer that will accept no less. Most often, I suppose, said abandonment arises from commercial or critical failures, which certainly describes my writing career. The cause of this, however, is not a failure of hard work or talent, but rather, as I'm painfully learning more and more under Master Yan's tutelage, that recurring inability to get out of my own way.

I trace this problem to various pernicious notions that have affected me from my wee years forward and have since become so entrenched in the tree branches of my brain that they feel as though they are an organic part of me. The first of these misconceptions is the notion that to rebel is to be free. Another is the inheritance of my father's need for the approval of others—in my case compounded by my need for *his* approval. A third is the desire not to compete with my father, primarily so as not to draw away from him the attention I know he so sorely needs. I know I need to jettison this baggage and that I've been carrying it too long. With that in mind, I decide to write a novel that is audacious in plot and avantgarde in style: precisely the kind of book I want to write regardless of convention or genre. Yes, I hope some readers like it, but what I really want is it to represent the best I can do, the kind of book *I myself* would really like to read if someone else wrote it. I start with the idea of two motorcycle riders being sucked aloft by a tornado over the Oklahoma panhandle—an image that just comes to me—and work backward from there. Who are they? Where are they going? Why are they on motorcycles? What will be their fate? My publisher nominates the novel, *A Cure for Gravity*, for a National Book Award. *The Sun-Sentinel* names it one of the ten best books of the year. *The Denver Post* says it has the best first sentence of any novel published in 2000.

One Saturday morning as I'm getting ready to teach my group tai chi class, my phone rings. I take the call in my kitchen in Boca Raton, watching my pet tarantula feast on a cricket. A heavily accented voice is on the other end of the line.

Is this the author of A Cure for Gravity?

I'm cautious in the face of this kind of accent, as my father is wont to play practical jokes sounding something like this and I suspect it may be him. I decide to play along, though with the requisite sardonic tone.

It is...

I received the book from the president of CBS. I have to say, you write like an angel.

Still thinking I'm indulging my father, I indulge the call just a moment longer.

Thank you. And you are?

This is Milos Forman calling.

THE MONK OF PARK AVENUE

I know the famous director primarily from *One Flew Over the Cuckoo's Nest* and *Amadeus,* and I'm sure my father (despite his ignorance of pop culture) knows him too. I'm on the verge of saying that I am Mickey Mouse, but the fact that I can't quite place the accent stops me. It isn't Russian-Jewish, nor Italian or French, my father's usual choices. I later learn it's Czech, of course, because this really *is* Milos Forman. Thankfully, I choose my next words carefully.

> *Does this call mean you would like to make a film of my book?*
>
> *I'm traveling to Europe tomorrow for a six-month stay. I'm going to take your book with me. If it blooms like a flower in my heart, the answer is yes. If it turns black and dies, the answer is no. I will call you upon my return.*

Forman goes and comes back, and he does call me. I go to see him at his home in Connecticut, and we spend most of the weekend discussing not only my novel, but literature in general, and of course, film. The famous man shares his views on the importance of story as we zoom around rural corners in his 911 Porsche and opines on point of view and character development in his kitchen in the company of his wife and their twin sons. In the end, and to my disappointment, he decides he is more compelled by a story about the artist Francisco Goya, which he cowrites and directs. This takes nothing away from the weekend experience, however, and I continue to ruminate upon his ideas for years; *A Cure for Gravity* is optioned twice more by other directors.

Next, I return to my crime-writing roots. Looking back, this seems a strange choice, maybe the last gasp of my pull to the genre, but nonetheless I write an unusual book called *Diamond Eye* about a United States Postal Inspector named

Max Diamond. I'm the first writer to choose this branch of law enforcement for their protagonist, probably because most writers don't consider the job sexy enough to sustain a series character—which is what I'm hoping Max will be. The trouble is, there is not any background available about what the job looks like, save for references to the service's Pony Express origins. In fact, inspectors are everywhere in post offices, often surveying the proceedings from lookout galleries that resemble giant ductwork with black windows.

I contact the service and am put in touch with the head of public relations to present my credentials as a writer interested in portraying the service accurately. There isn't much interest until I take a bit of a stronger tack.

I'm trying to do something good for both of us here. You can give me the inside scoop, or you can deny me and hope I don't get it all wrong and make you look bad in my book.

I'm invited to postal inspector school to view the crime lab they share with other agencies and ride with local inspectors to get a sense of the daily routine of the job. All this leads me to conclude I have made a good choice in bringing the service to life through fiction. The mandate of these inspectors is quite broad, meaning they get to investigate anything connected with the US Mail and these are the days when the mail still connects the world.

Walking around the forensics lab up in the northeast in the company of the inspector in charge of congressional and public affairs, I come across a door with a little window in it. Passing by, I peer in and see an inspector sitting in front of a television monitor, a stack of tapes beside him. To say he looks glum is to say a turkey hates Thanksgiving. I'm curious.

What's going on in there.

My minder shrus.

Nothing.

No, really. What's that guy doing in a room by himself and why does he look like he'd rather be hammering nails through his hands?

Bad things go through the mail. Someone has to look and see how bad they are.

There is something about the way he says this that makes me feel like I want to vomit. Without asking permission, I push open the door and step into the room. The watcher is slow to climb to his feet, but when he sees his boss in the door frame, he moves more quickly. My minder barks an order.

Turn it off.

The inspector does, but not before I get a glimpse of something terrible involving children. I have no idea what to say. All I can manage is,

I'm sorry.

Back in the hallway, we walk in silence for a while.

You shouldn't have gone in.

I'm sorry I did. I'll likely never forget that scene.

That may be the worst job on the force. Nobody can take it for very long. We rotate through. He'll spend a week at most doing that. Usually less.

Back home, it's not only the scene that plagues me but the guy sitting alone in that room being forced to watch things nobody should ever, ever see. I tap into my visceral outrage and disgust and use them as an engine. I give my fictional inspector the same feelings I have, the same feelings I saw on the real inspector's face. During the next year, I live the life of an inspector who takes down a kiddie-porn and snuff-film ring. While I'm writing it, I take four showers a day, and even so, I don't feel clean. The cost of writing this book is unacceptably high.

The presence of my young son, Tasman, makes these feelings even stronger. He's born in 2000 and is nothing but a great joy to me. Spending time with him makes me ever more keenly aware of how I want to be the right role model; I want to spend my time on the highest possible things I feel I can do with my life. I finish the book and it garners some awards. I even win recognition from the National Center for Missing and Exploited Children for shining a light on human trafficking. I accept the award, but onstage can't shake the feeling that I have flat-out lost my way. I don't want to write about the worst of people; I want to write about the best of people. I don't want to swim in a swamp of deviance; I want to fly between clouds of enlightened possibilities and positive futures. I see what's wrong with the world very clearly, I just don't want to revel in it. I speak with my agent about the fact that ever since Thomas Harris wrote *The Silence of the Lambs* back in 1988, the bar has been so high for turning out disgusting deviants who can out-Hannibal Hannibal Lecter that no crime writer can hope to hit the big time without going down heretofore utterly unthinkable paths. I'm not willing to do that ever again. Not again. That is the moment I decide crime writing is not for me, and that chronicling Hell is not why I became a writer. I may have *found* a real-life Master Po, but I have not yet *become* a real-life master of anything.

I have to figure out a way to conflate my spiritual quest with my creative work. Books like *Diamond Eye* are not that way.

So I change direction. My next book is one of service, a nonfiction work about suffering in America called *The Truth About Chronic Pain*. In it, I juxtapose the epidemic of unnecessary misery around the country with the burgeoning abuse of opioid narcotic medications. I present pain as a psychosocial phenomenon as opposed to merely a medical problem. The book becomes a hardcover bestseller. Next, I'm ready to meld my interest in Chinese culture and martial arts into a new kind of work altogether. I call it *kung fu noir*, a melding of martial arts, history, fantasy, and Chinese history. A big ad in *Rolling Stone* magazine spreads the catchy phrase.

Keen to try a different way to get my work out there, I work with a New Hampshire publisher of niche texts about martial arts. This turns out to be a pretty terrible idea, as the publisher has no idea how to market fiction and gets neither exposure nor distribution for my work. All the same, I'm excited about the series protagonist, Xenon Pearl, the neurosurgeon vigilante who entered my head in Hong Kong. He is a creative sociopath who hears voices in his head and talks to ghosts, but he also has some fans and some detractors. He's good for a couple of outings in the novels *The Cutting Season* and *Quiet Teacher*, but the real fun comes when that immortal brother and sister I conceived in Hong Kong come alive on the pages of *The Crocodile and the Crane*. Presciently, as it turns out, they battle a pandemic that is Nature's way of punishing us for having too many babies and for doing all that we have done to her.

That latter novel allows me to dance with Deep Ecology—the notion of Planet Earth as a superorganism that acts to protect itself—originally conceived in the 1970s by Norwegian philosopher Arne Naess and popularized by the British writer James Lovelock in his books about Gaia. I find it increasingly tempting to see human beings as a cancer on the face of the planet, behaving just as cancer cells do by reproducing at unsustainable levels, physically destroying the circulatory system and bones of the host (think ruining the oceans with plastic, fracking, drilling, poisoning creeks, streams, rivers, lakes, and clear-cutting forests), and outcompeting all other cells in the body (think the Sixth Great Extinction). The novel also allows me to advance the Daoist prescription for our planet as a coherent philosophy that unites the way of nature with the way of man and the larger forces at work in the universe. Daoism, it turns out, was the world's first coherent conservation system—the origin of what it means to use resources in a sustainable fashion and to live in harmony with nature. The more I learn about it, the more I find I want to devote myself to it.

Meeting Master Yan, it turns out, was just the catalyst I needed to begin to focus all the disparate threads of my life. Under his tutelage, and more precisely under the umbrella of Daoism, I find ever more meaning in the things I do. I'm able to see glimpses of what lies beneath the surface of the world, and thereby to begin to realize the ambition that first occurred to me as a child. Meaning brings power and power brings focus. I feel not only suffused with purpose but eager to engage the multiple opportunities to deepen my understanding of the world and share what I learn.

CHAPTER 5

HISTORY, CULTURE, AND FISTS

I t's March of 2006 and I'm in Beijing with Master Yan. We are at the very start of an ambitious tour of famous Daoist sites across the country, students in tow. The first morning of the trip, the group heavy with jetlag, Master Yan appears at our hotel breakfast and announces he has a family emergency, appoints me "tour captain," and departs. We are all stunned. I am especially at sea; I know few particulars of our itinerary and have none of the necessary contacts. We manage to proceed thanks to the capable work of a charming Beijing-based tour guide, who orchestrates our transfers and hires local guides for day excursions. The highlight of the trip for many of us is a visit to Wudang Mountain, a legendary Daoist peak known to all students of Chinese philosophy and martial arts. No thanks to a flat tire and a road closure, we arrive at the mountain's base village several hours behind schedule. Our local guide, a wiry goat of a man who has spent his life on the mountain, appears and shakes his head.

*No time to climb the mountain. Dark coming soon. No
facilities at the top. No place for tourists. No rooms. No
toilets. Too cold now. Snow coming.*

My group goes nuts. The younger, more macho members
of the crew protest that they have traveled 10,000 miles for
this particular pilgrimage, have been looking forward to it all
their lives, and won't be denied the summit. I try to explain
this to the guide.

*Sorry. Take too many hours to climb the famous path. You
can take cable car. Tram. Very fast.*

*Yes, but that's not climbing the mountain. It's kind
of cheating.*

Only way. So sorry you so late.

The ladies on our tour agree and head off toward the
tram station, but the young men in the crowd start to grunt
like drunken soldiers, hammer their fists, stomp their feet,
and insist on the climb. Trying to forestall a mutiny, I ask the
guide another question.

*Is there not another way up the mountain that is a bit
faster? I know the tourist path is paved and scenic and
safe and beautiful but surely not everyone uses the
same way up.*

The guy shakes his head.

Only one way.

*But a mountain is a three-dimensional thing. Surely local
people don't use the tourist path. I bet your mayor doesn't
even allow that. When you go to the top or when work is
needed on the temple up there, how do local people climb?*

Our Beijing guide chimes in, waving her official government badge. At length the local guide relents.

Of course there is another way, but it is not for you. The path is steep and there is ice and snow. There are no guardrails and nothing for you to hold on to. There are places where the path is very narrow, and we have to press against the rock wall and go one by one. It's a five-thousand-foot drop and I can't be responsible for your safety. If something happens, there is no rescue available.

The young bucks in my group look at me expectantly. Concerned at my lack of mountaineering experience, but not wanting to lose face, I agree. The Beijing guide says she will keep me company, and we head off. I'm pretty sure I've made a mistake within the first ten minutes. I'm not well-suited to altitude due to asthma and more. Even so, we navigate the narrows successfully, bodies pressed against the granite as anticipated. I choose not to look down. Halfway up the icy, muddy path, it begins to snow. The sky darkens. The local guide looks at the sky, looks at his watch, turns to address us.

Have to go faster. Have to run. If we don't reach the summit before five o'clock, the tram will close for the day and we won't be able to get down.

I'm going as fast as I can but I'm not capable of literally running up the mountain in the cold air. I don't want to seem like a weak old man to my students, but I really am slowing them down. (I will later come to realize that my heart is the problem, damaged by some medication prescribed to me to help the inflammation in my knees.) The Beijing guide takes pity on me.

I'll go back down with you.

Feeling all the worse for her indulgence, we reluctantly descend. Our new mission is to get to the tram station and convince the operators to send the car up so my students won't be stranded in the cold. Once again approaching the scary narrows, I spy a lone figure coming up the path toward us. Daylight is fading to dusk and the figure is far away, but I can't imagine whoever it is will make it to the summit before dark. As the three of us draw closer, I see that the figure is a woman, and that she is carrying a wooden yoke across her shoulders. Suspended from the yoke are two tin pails. Nearer still, I discern that the pails are full of bricks. She's bringing them up to help repair the walls of the summit temple, my guide explains.

As luck would have it, we intersect at the tightest point on the path. There is no room for all of us, and the woman gestures impatiently for us to get out of the way. The guide and I press ourselves against the rock wall again. Grumbling, the woman passes us, her heavy pails swinging gently. As she does, I notice she's quite old. I'm curious about her and address my guide.

How old do you think she is?

The most direct thing to do is to ask the old lady and that is exactly what the young woman does. The reply comes quickly.

I'm ninety-one.

I'm stunned.

And she's still carrying bricks up the mountain?

The guide pats my arm.

Don't feel bad. You come from a different world. A different life. She has been going up and down this path every day of her life since she was three years old.

Still, I can't help but try to wrap my mind around the unimaginable suffering endured by the Chinese people, and the deprivation and challenges they have become accustomed to facing and surmounting. My conclusion is that America must never go to war with China. Despite the Great Depression, the Dustbowl Days and the sacrifices of two world wars, our current population is just not used to Chinese levels of sacrifice and deprivation. When we get back to town, the Beijing guide sends one last tram car up to bring my crew down. As it ends up, I'm the only one who never does reach the summit of Wudang Mountain.

Perhaps someday.

———————

A few years later, I'm in China again with Master Yan and some other students. We're down south this time, in Bamboo County, Guangdong Province, visiting the small village where the master's mother was born. The Chinese name for this county is Guangning and because of its tropical beauty and luxuriant foliage, it has been described as a pearl in an oyster of greenery. It's also an area known for the special tea residents make from bamboo leaves. I find such things fascinating, having become a full-blown Sinophile and embracing traditional Chinese history and culture for a better, deeper understanding of how Daoism arose and how it still manifests in Asia. Strictly speaking, the so-called tea is actually an infusion; true tea comes only from the plant Camellia sinensis. The infusion I'm drinking is said to cure all kinds of ills. It tastes bitter compared to both the Taiwanese and Fujian

Province high-mountain oolongs and richly layered Yunnan Province pu'erh I've come to love. The latter style of tea, dried into hard cakes, was originally conceived to survive the journey, by horse and camel, across the ancient Silk Roads all the way to the courts of Europe and on to the Middle East. In the old days, such tea was worth more than its weight in gold and prized almost as highly as that other most coveted Cathay export, silk. Even now, fine Chinese tea is far from cheap.

We drop in on a relative of Master Yan's on his mother's side, a bonesetter. Bone setting is not chiropractic but rather an ancient and vaunted art, a branch of traditional Chinese medicine (TCM) that deals with the effects of trauma, aging, and disease on the hard structure of the human body. Associating it with TCM requires the disclaimer that there really is no such thing. The term is an artificial construct— one of many the Chinese Communist Party employs to homogenize, manipulate, and control the population— designed to nationalize, if not globalize, indigenous Chinese medical practices for commercial reasons.

The fact is, China has only recently had the infrastructure to support any kind of widespread, coherent system of healthcare, and even now, that infrastructure is not terribly effective. It is, after all, a vast country with a huge array of ethnicities and traditions. There are hundreds of thousands of villages in China, many of which are associated with either a single family or a small group of families. Many, many families have their own healthcare traditions going back hundreds, if not thousands, of years. These traditions involve herbs, potions, *qigong*, and, more rarely, bone setting. To have the skill to align and mend broken bones and heal traumatic injuries is a highly prized skill, and rightly so.

Master Yan's cousin has a clinic, which is a simple place with a basic reception area and a couple of treatment rooms. While we are there, a teenage boy is brought in by his family. He has been in a motorcycle accident and his shattered left arm, having been run over by a car, dangles by his side, glistening bones protruding. He is in shock, pallid, sweating, and dizzy. Back home, he would be taken to an emergency room in an ambulance. Another of Master Yan's students, an anesthesiologist, expresses his doubts.

That kid needs a hospital right now.

Master Yan responds.

This is the hospital.

Apparently unimpressed by the injury, the bonesetter waves him in. The kid can barely stand by himself. The first thing the bonesetter does is stick in a couple of acupuncture needles. Within moments, the boy visibly relaxes. His breathing slows, he stops sweating, and he settles down. My friend the allopathic physician can't believe his eyes. Of course, he's not the only one who thinks the Western way is the only way. My own physician father is an example of someone whose experiences in China changed his way at looking at so-called "alternative" medicine. Since the system is thousands of years old compared to allopathy's short and highly checkered career, it's not clear the comparison is quite accurate, especially given what my father witnessed on his own trip.

It was decades earlier than my visit, and he was accompanying Averell Harriman on a relationship-building delegation. Harriman, son of a railroad tycoon, forty-eighth Governor of New York, one-time presidential candidate, purveyor of political wisdom, and diplomat extraordinaire, was wont to have such meetings in politically volatile parts of the world, sallying forth as a special envoy, the better to build a foundation upon which later alliances will stand. Sometimes, in his later years, he took my father both as doctor and advisor. As part of their high-end meetings, and to put their best foot forward and impress their American visitors with Chinese culture, science, and healthcare, my father is treated to a bit of open-heart surgery at a Chinese hospital. What made the experience most memorable for my father is that the procedure is done without anesthesia. While they are cutting her chest in half and working on her heart, the female patient was awake and talking, allegedly having only been given acupuncture for pain and a Valium for anxiety.

Critics of my father's widely published account of the proceedings pointed out that, with the chest open, the lungs lack the pressure differential to function properly and there was no way such a patient could breathe without a ventilator, much less talk to visiting dignitaries. They claimed my father had been duped, that the head of the real patient was actual secreted on the lower level of the treatment table, and that the woman who was speaking as a stand-in—a sham— overlain on a magician's table. The whole event, those same critics asserted, was something a Vegas performer could duplicate in, um, a heartbeat—a piece of medical sleight of hand designed to fool a famous Western cardiologist and his traveling companions. My father was incensed by this coverage. I'm not a rube, he says. I'm a heart specialist and I know what I saw.

We may never know exactly what he saw, but here at the Bamboo County clinic, I get to see some pretty miraculous Chinese medicine myself up close and personal and I find myself believing his account. There are no cameras, no political angle, or any eager debunkers waiting in the wings to disparage a system some still view as junk science. Before the bonesetter can get to work, my physician friend intervenes.

Aren't you going to take an X-ray?

Don't need one.

Well, could you do one anyway? After all, you have a machine.

The bonesetter shrugs and takes the boy for a film. He gets a couple of angles and reviews them with my friend, who feels vindicated in his earlier assessment of the seriousness of the injury.

He's going to need a drawer full of pins to hold together those bits of bone and set that compound fracture.

The bonesetter seems not to think so. He places his hands on the boy's shoulder and works his way down the arm. As far as I can see, his touch is light as a feather. He circumvents the protruding bone, his fingers trailing the boy's flesh, his eyes closed like a lover. Master Yan narrates.

He's figuring out what to do. He can feel every tiny break and how to fix it. He will go one by one until the arm is perfect again.

The bonesetter carefully cleans the protruding bone and the skin around it, then makes another pass, top to bottom. This time, he is clearly applying pressure, because we see the contour of the arm shifting. Gradually, the protruding bone disappears. The boy remains relaxed and in no apparent discomfort. Over and over the bonesetter's fingers run over the boy's flesh, pressing, pulling, lightly squeezing. My friend's expression says he is witnessing voodoo.

> Could we have another X-ray, please? I'd like to see what you did.

The bonesetter applies a poultice first. It looks like country mustard without the seeds. He's stern when addressing the boy.

> Don't let it dry. After one week of this one, come back and I will give you another one that dries harder and holds everything in place. Two weeks with that and you're done.

He has the boy repeat the protocol.
Master Yan whispers to me.

> The herbs are a secret family recipe. The ingredients are critically important.

My physician friend repeats his request for another X-ray, then examines the films.

> Look at these seams. He's got all the pieces back in place so perfectly tight, I can't even be sure I see the cracks. Frankly, this puts Western medicine utterly to shame. We could never do something like this. We'd have to totally put him under to operate; he'd be full of pins and entry incisions.

Master Yan interjects.

> This kind of thing takes many years to learn to do. Generation after generation, my mom's family passes it down. When they stop doing it, the knowledge will be lost. This is our history. It is our tradition.

An undercurrent of history and tradition underpins everything I do with Master Yan and everything I learn from him. The same could be said about my life before him, of the thousands of years of Jewish history, the culture, the language, the suffering, isolation, combativeness, guilt, preoccupation with justice and intellectual inquiry, and tragically the monotheistic world view that leads people to feel special enough to justify destroying each other and the whole world. Before I met Master Yan, those aforementioned forces were as invisible to me as water is to a fish. After years with him, however, they are all too evident and clear.

The most relevant part of Master Yan's personal history may not be his distant lineage but his recent past. He is literally the product of Chinese eugenics. The same Chinese government that destroyed millions of lives with the inaptly named Cultural Revolution understood the benefits of selective breeding long before our own government sterilized a certain group of African Americans and put them in supervisory care facilities. In Master Yan's case, the Chinese government brings together two august families, one the descendants of far north rulers, including recent war heroes, and the other the elite of the south, all bonesetters. His parents are both academics, stars of physics and engineering, one working for the government designing silent drives for submarines, the other working in the field of missile telemetry and guidance. How exactly they are brought together, Master Yan does not tell me, but he makes it clear that it was done deliberately, as is so much in modern China, where individuality is a liability and privacy a memory. In short, my teacher is a genius for a reason, and the Chinese government is making more and more like him even without cloning and recombinant technology.

A few hours after witnessing the bone setting, Master Yan and I mark my ten-year anniversary of study in a large, private, upstairs room in a local restaurant. We share our table with his students and a few of my own. There is music and enough food, all tastes varied and wonderful, to qualify for a banquet. We are guests of the town's vice mayor, in part because foreigners are shown a good time, but more because Master Yan is a local celebrity. Everyone is drunk, including Master Yan, who can hold his liquor as well as anyone I have ever met but is, nonetheless, mostly staring at his soup.

Thinking back on our first meal together in the restaurant in Hollywood, Florida, I'm struck by how long it has taken me to get here, how many thousands of hours of dedicated work have passed, and how seismic the shift in my priorities and worldview has been. Overcome with gratitude, I stand for a toast. There are no glasses and no spoons either, so I tap my teacup with chopsticks. At first, nobody notices. They are all drunk. Nonetheless, I speak out and I speak loudly.

> Tonight makes it exactly ten years since I started training with Master Yan. I just want to take this moment to thank him for forgiving me my arrogance and ignorance, for sticking with me despite my blundering physical ineptitude, for seeing past my cultural, personal, and political transgressions enough to continue to have me as his student. Nine grateful bows to you, Shifu.

There is a scattering of applause, mostly from my own students. I'm not entirely sure Master Yan heard me until he mutters, into his bowl.

> Took me ten years to trust you.

In martial arts, the term "form" denotes a piece of choreography featuring martial techniques strung together. Forms are memory tools; they help us remember moves the way songs help us remember words. Some forms have other purposes, too, such as changing the body or conveying a hierarchy of principles. In most martial art systems, we begin with a simple sequence, then learn progressively longer and more challenging ones as our mastery grows. In authentic Chen-style tai chi, the original and once-secret open-hand (weaponless) form of the now-popular art is long, complex, and takes years to learn properly. The second form most commonly taught teaches the *jian*, or double-edged straight sword, a thrusting weapon that strengthens the wrist, develops hand-eye coordination, and cultivates the ability to project and sense energy. There is another open-hand form and there are other weapons forms, too. I like to practice all of them outside in the park, even in the steamy South Florida summer.

My favorite park borders the Intracoastal Waterway and is home to a population of homeless people who sleep under the bridge at the park's south end, high atop an inconspicuous concrete buttress. One afternoon, while practicing the *jian* in the park, a thunderstorm rolls in. Florida is the lightning strike capital of the world, so we make haste for the shelter of the bridge. The storm hits with ferocious intensity. Daoists love weather as nature in performance mode and I relish the jagged bolts of lightning over the water, the palm trees curtsying to their mother, the wind rippling the brine. Then a bolt strikes too close for comfort. The next one strikes the bridge superstructure. The air turns a strange shade of brown, something I have never seen before.

The smell of ozone permeates the air. A group of homeless people cowering beneath the buttress shriek in terror. Having shared this organic, life-threatening moment with these folks, and having retained some composure in the face of it whilst everyone else lost theirs, a certain grudging respect is born, a bond created. They come to know me and I them. They accept my presence and I sometime even serve as an arbiter in their disputes. All in all, it's a happy arrangement.

A few weeks after finding this new park, Master Yan comes to see me. We establish ourselves at a picnic table. I stretch and warm up for a lesson while my teacher drinks tea. A homeless man wearing a ball cap that says "Inky" appears and seems curious about the proceedings.

What are you doing?

My teacher looks uncomfortable, so I'm the one to answer.

Chinese exercises.

No, you're not, you're doing martial arts. I was in the special forces in Vietnam. I could kick your ass right now.

I'm sure. Please don't.

Master Yan looks alarmed, but Inky wanders off. Out of the corner of my eye, I see him head off to the bridge. I go back to talking to Master Yan. Because of the angle of his next approach, I don't see Inky again until I smell him close to me and see Master Yan's eyes fly open. I turn just in time to catch a sucker punch to the back of my head. Inky's punch is ripe with momentum, and my defensive technique is just right, lifting him off the ground and sending him flying past the picnic table. He goes so fast and so far, he reaches the concrete seawall along the edge of the Intracoastal

Waterway. He collapses there and the sound of his skull hitting the concrete is one of the worst noises I've heard.

Master Yan and I rush over. Inky is unresponsive. I search his neck for a pulse. Master Yan is concerned.

> *Is he dead? If he is, you could push him into the water so it will look like he drowned.*

> *I'm not pushing anyone anywhere. Besides, he's not dead. There's a pulse.*

I slap Inky's cheeks. Finally, his eyes flutter open and he looks up at me.

> *What happened?*

> *You fell.*

A couple of weeks later, I'm practicing in the same park and Inky rides up to me again.

> *What's that you're doing?*

> *We already had this discussion. You told me how you were in the special forces and that you could kill me. Then you sucker punched me in the back of the head.*

> *I did?*

> *Yes.*

> *What happened?*

> *It didn't go well for you.*

He scratches himself and shuffles his feet and comes up with something to say.

> *I'm sorry.*

> *I know you are. If you want to talk to me, come back when you're sober.*

THE MONK OF PARK AVENUE

Inky does not remember flying through the air and cracking his head on a concrete seawall, but references to sobriety stick with him. I know this because a week later, he shows up early one morning looking hungry. I know he will drink whatever money I give him, so I go to a local bagel place and bring him back breakfast. As he eats, he tells me his story.

> I wasn't in the special forces. I was a trunk driver and crane operator, unloading boats along the Mekong River during the Vietnam war. When I got home, I became a drunk. I lost everything. My family, my job. I have a daughter somewhere. I don't remember where. Nobody talks to me anymore. All I have left is this blue plastic watch, my bike, and three teeth.

Two weeks later, Inky disappears. When I ask a few of the other guys about him, they tell me he is dead. Hit by a truck while riding his bike, they say. I take this news kind of hard. I think about how fragile life is and how fleeting. I think about the effectiveness of the art Master Yan has taught me and about how many different ways there are to put Daoism into practice besides physical violence. I don't regret defending myself from being punched in the head, but I do realize that Inky's fall very well could have killed him. He really did travel quite a distance and hit his head hard. Somehow this event concretizes things for me, makes me feel them in a gritty way. Master Yan is proud of how well I did with my defense and tells others about it, but I feel somehow ashamed, as if hurting another person, no matter what their intentions toward me, is not why I'm in the game. What I really want is to use my training to go ever deeper into the nature of things, into the workings of the universe.

CHAPTER 6

THE PATH FINALLY CLEAR

The coach of the Yale swim team once told me that the only reason he kept me on the squad was as a mascot to make the other guys laugh. The rectification of Daoist practice changes me physically to the point that I'm nobody's mascot. I become flexible in ways I never imagined I could be and develop the internal connections needed to make power and apply martial arts techniques. Physical results are obvious but mental ones less clear. After thousands of hours of Master Yan's standing pole meditation, I begin to think that awareness is as much a matter of filtration as of heightened perception. I come to understand that the brain's primary job is not computation but limitation, reducing the overwhelming amount of information bombarding us at every moment to a manageable level.

What information do I mean? Cosmic rays sending particles through our skin; the frequencies of light issuing from the sun; the currents, tiny storms, and vortices of the air at our cutaneous boundaries; plants sighing as they grow; rocks groaning as tectonic plates shift below them; the maelstrom of pheromones released by housecats and breeding-aged members of the opposite sex; the fecal emanations of rats in the walls; the veritable circus of bacterial effluents in the air around us. If we are aware of all these things at every moment, how could we ever get anything done?

Dao itself is ineffable; the greatest sages say so. Speaking of it, we fail to define it, and in defining it, we limit it in a way that is immediately incomplete and incorrect. We have only language to share ideas like this with each other, but language is not enough. So it is for Dao and so it is for *qi*, the life force or vital essence that is such a quintessentially Chinese concept I'm not sure Westerners can really grasp it. How does one translate, or explain to foreigners, something that has grown like a flower in the once mineral-rich soil of the Motherland? I'm not sure such an enterprise is possible and I'm not sure it matters.

Dr. Shin Lin does. He is a researcher at the University of California, Irvine, and he is convinced there is a reality to *qi* that can be scientifically substantiated. Standing in his lab, in the company of a documentary film team I have put together to make a film about tai chi and related subjects, part of me admires his quixotic pursuit and part of me worries about a Chinese professor's need to validate something so quintessentially Chinese in Western terms. Dr. Lin shows me a variety of experiments he is doing to qualify the nature of *qi* and quantify how much is present in a person. He has an idea to make the film better.

Would you be a test subject?

My producer nods vigorously, agreeing that this will make good television and so I'm wired up to a machine that measures galvanic skin response. Dr. Lin explains why.

Qi could be electricity generated across cell membranes. Of course, it could also be ultra-low frequency sound or even the information contained in our DNA.

My cameramen capture me sitting with wires attached, showing the screen as I meditate. Electrical spikes an order of magnitude larger than any other test subject has managed appear. Dr. Lin has people running in and out from all over the lab, even from down the hall, because he is so excited. I have no idea what any of this means.

Another machine comes next. Simpler, but more radical, at least for a guy who does still photography. Dr. Lin gives me the details.

This is a very special kind of Japanese camera. It is designed to measure a single photon, the basic unit of light. Now, light behaves as both a particle and a wave. We are open to the possibility that qi and light are one and the same.

He rolls a thick rubber sleeve over my arm. It reaches from my fingertips all the way to my shoulder and reminds me of the sort of protection I used at veterinary school to examine a pregnant cow, though more snug, jet-black, and completely light-tight.

The point of the sleeve is to create unimaginable darkness around your hand. Feel the cradle? Put your wrist in it and point your palm away from you. Good. Now the sensor is aimed at your palm, at the acupuncture point called Laogong, also known as Pericardium 8. As amazingly sensitive as this camera is, it is no more so than the human eye, which can also detect a single photon if given enough time to adapt to the darkness. Sometimes, when we think we see something in the night and tell ourselves we're imagining it, we're not. We're just seeing something very, very faint. I've wired the sensor to a speaker, so every time it detects a single photon, you will hear a beep. We want to see if someone like you, who has worked with energy and meditation intensively, can emit light from your palm. If you can, it might help explain qi transmission, which is the way energy healers in China and elsewhere are able to work their magic even without physically touching the patient. Ok, the technicians are ready so what I'd like you to do is imagine doing tai chi. Concentrate on your hand. See if you can mentally guide your energy to the palm point.

I do as he asks. At first, nothing happens, but then the machine beeps. I try not to let the sound distract me. I keep my eyes closed and do more of what I have been doing. Another beep. I'm emitting light from my palm inside a light-tight box. I continue the exercise. Very soon, the occasional beeps become a continuous drone, signifying a veritable beam of light hitting the sensor. Dr. Lin is so happy, he claps his hands. It might be the film footage of this strange event that convinces Detroit Public Television to create a national show based on my documentary called *Longevity Tai Chi*, which runs for three years and reaches nearly 200 million viewers.

It is March of 2012 and I've come to Southern China for a particular reason. I am here to be ordained a Daoist monk. Pouring sweat, I kneel before a Daoist altar. Spring has come to Guangzhou, the southern Chinese city formerly known as Canton, and the heavy black robes I wear would be better suited to an expedition to Everest. I chant Mandarin phrases I don't fully understand, my fellow monks helping me as they can. Some of them ring bells. All around us are wooden statues honoring city gods, deities of Chinese history, and even Buddha and Guanyin. This is the Pure Yang Temple (*Chun Yang Guan*), part of the Complete Truth/Ultimate Reality (*Quanzhen*) sect that arose later than some other sects and at a time when Buddhism was gaining ground in the imperial court and Daoism needed to attract followers with promises of spiritual benefits not included in the original, shamanistic Daoist philosophy. In addition to my robes, I wear a rectangular hat accented with a flat tab of jade right above my third eye.

Presiding over the ordination festivities is the temple's chief monk and abbot, Pan Chongxian, a man I observe occupies the traditional role of the Daoist master by advising politicians and luminaries. Here, as elsewhere in China, I see blacked-out limousines in the temple parking lot. Communist Party functionaries seek Abbot Pan's advice on such questions like what might be a propitious time for them to make a predatory career move, have their daughter marry the son of a rival politician in order to forge an alliance, or undertake a risky surgery at this particular phase of the moon, stars, and the Five Elements.

The temple was once in a sylvan setting. Not now. Urban Guangzhou has expanded, growing closer and closer until it reaches the temple's grounds. Parts of the property were subsumed, many of the structures degraded or destroyed outright. Guangzhou's garment district—one of the largest in the world—all but surrounds the place now, motivating Abbot Pan to lead a long-term restoration project aimed at restoring the grounds to their former bucolic glory. His own quarters are modest but since he receives no fees for his services and asks for donations to the temple instead, he has a formidable art collection. Comprised of paintings, sculptures, jade, manuscripts, and scrolls, it eventually requires its own standalone gallery.

My ordination ceremony is lengthy. I worry I will pass out in the heat. Not so for Abbot Pan, whose acolytes attend him with fans that look like giant bamboo lollipops. His expression is impassive most of the day, but toward the end, when I kneel before him in obeisance, he favors me with a smile that makes me suddenly understand why Catholics love their popes and orthodox Jews their famous rabbis. He has a beatific energy. I bow to him nine times. My tears flow even as his gaze asks.

What are you doing here, you crazy American?

Abbot Pan bestows upon me a unique Daoist name, and I'm honored by it. All the same, out of loyalty, I subsequently choose to go by the name Master Yan has given me. Master Yan comes out of the *Shangqing* Daoist tradition, which is older, more philosophical, arguably less politically inclusive, and focused a bit more tightly on self-cultivation. I'm singularly blessed to have these two masters in two distinct lineages, but at one point, I express to both my masters that I feel an imposter.

> *I'm not Chinese and am not allowed to permanently reside at the monastery. I won't be cleaning and sweeping and cooking like the others.*

Both explain the same thing.

You were drawn to Daoism as a child. You've had no support in following this path, not from your family or friends, culture, or surrounding society. In fact, you were likely ridiculed or at least misunderstood until you found what you were after. You didn't try and change anybody's mind about anything or get into arguments about your choice, you just kept going. Most of the other monks at the monastery are young men from wealthy families. Unlike Buddhists, Daoists are not renunciates and Chinese culture is such that children, particularly sons, are required to support their families. Nobody can be here unless his contribution to the family wealth can be spared for their seven-year stint. These men may clean latrines and garden and run prayer and physical exercise sessions, but at night they strap on their Rolexes and drive their Mercedes Benzes home to their wives and children. Your path was not so easy, and it was walked on the other side of the world, mostly alone. You're not alone anymore. Take what you can do with language and media and share Daoist ideas with the world. That's your Daoist mission and it is every bit is as important as sweeping, cooking, cleaning, meditating, or conducting rituals. These ideas are universal. As much as you love Chinese culture and history and arts, Daoism is not just about China. It applies, it works, everywhere on Earth, in any language, and for every living creature. Daoism offers solutions to the problems faced by humankind present.

I want to tell my masters that I am not who they think I am—that I'm here in the arts and under the umbrella of the philosophy because it is the only way I can make sense of the world, the only way I can keep my equilibrium, the only way I can grow. They would just shrug if I said any of this, for they know that the philosophy and its practices mean different things to different people, offering the puzzle piece that completes the set for many different situations and many different lives. This may be due to what Daoist scholar Louis Komjathy calls Daoism's permeability, which requires the through passage of both philosophical ideas and ongoing observations of nature. Similarly, there is a permeability to the human body, which is mostly water and requires water to pass through it constantly in order to survive, intimately connected to the natural world. Small wonder Daoist masters exhort us to emulate the way water seeps and flows without effort and often to dramatic effect in both taking and giving life.

Back at home, my robes suit me in ways that go far beyond tailoring. Despite the heat, later, elsewhere, even in the cold, standing at my father's gravesite and shoveling dirt onto his coffin, they feel right to me. Comfortable. Appropriate.

A student asks me a question.

> Did you really have to go and become a monk to live a Daoist life? I mean, what's that all about?
>
> I didn't do it because it would help me live a Daoist life. A monk is his actions, not his clothing. I just enjoy being part of a special community. I enjoy conveying clearly to the world that I am committed to these ideas, this way of life, these values, and these practices.

I go back to Abbot Pan a year later and the year after that. I spend more time with him and gain a government certification that is officially stamped and allows me to legally conduct Daoist ceremonies. I gain a Daoist passport as well, with Master Pan's imprimatur and a photo of my face. This additional government document ensures that wherever I travel in China, any Daoist temple will give me refuge and provide room and board. Pan's adjutant, Master Che Gao Fei, also teaches me more Daoist rituals, including secret bows. I have only the faintest hints, at that time, that soon Pan and Che and all other Buddhist and Daoist monks, priests, ministers, rabbis, and preachers will all be completely disenfranchised—some even running for their lives—as Chinese leader Xi Jinping launches a campaign to extirpate from China anything that isn't his brand of communism.

In 2013, I publish the book *Tai Chi: The Perfect Exercise* to give voice to Master Yan's view of the art and its history, applications, and Daoist dimensions. In part because of this book, I'm invited to give the opening and closing speeches at the 2014 International Tai Chi Symposium in Louisville, Kentucky. I'm given a place on the dais with the heads of five tai chi families visiting from China, an honor I most definitely don't deserve. My TV show stops airing that year but garners me a Hollywood award for martial arts in media. Bruce Lee's goddaughter, Diana Lee Inosanto, presents the award. In my acceptance speech, I pay homage to not only Bruce Lee but David Carradine for his role in *Kung Fu*. After the speech, a woman approaches the table.

> Congratulations on the award. And thanks for mentioning David Carradine. Most people don't talk about him anymore.

> Actually, I wrote an obituary for him. I think it was for The Huffington Post but it might have been for the South Florida Sun-Sentinel. I just wrote about how important he was to so many people of my generation. I also wrote how he was a particular inspiration to me, bringing alive not only the martial arts but a culture and a way of looking

at things. I feel honored that he also won this same award years ago.

The woman bursts into tears.

Thank you! He was my father.

As a follow-up to the book on tai chi, I write a novel called *YIN: A Love Story* in which the great sage, Laozi, falls for the embodiment of female energy, a giant turtle. The fruit of more than twenty years of thoughtful crafting, *YIN* is an adult fairy tale, an adventure, a romance. I write it with my son in mind, not that it is a children's book but rather imagining that someday, when he is past the stage of teen rebellion and begins to see his father in a different light, the book will be his entre into Daoist thinking. I'm very aware that nobody has written anything else quite like it.

That's true and is the good news, says my literary agent, Sterling Lord. You are sole owner of whatever literary category this may be. The bad news, he goes on, is that nobody else is writing anything like what you're writing, so no publisher knows how to sell it. My good friend, the writer Tom Peek, tells me *YIN* is the most important book he has read in an age. Tom lives in Hawaii and is dedicated in the deepest possible way to preserving and celebrating Polynesian culture. My other good writer friend, Dennis O'Flaherty, does not care for the book at all. He is a professor trained at Oxford and Harvard.

Fiction shouldn't have a message. If you want to send a message, call Western Union.

I'm pretty startled by this.

Wait. Isn't the whole point of story to say something, reveal some deeper meaning to life? Isn't story the most effective way we have to speak the truth to each other?

Nope. Novels are entertainment, pure and simple.

I have to say I think you're dead wrong. Who says entertainment can't also have something to say? It seems to me as if you're dismissing the entire idea of literature along with the field of literary criticism.

More importantly, although I don't get into this with Dennis, he is dismissing the critical value of story in the development of language across the span of human history. By my lights, language developed because a proto-human monkey saw a leopard sneaking up on one of his friends, issued a cry the other monkey recognized as a warning, and spurred his friend to leap to safety at the last moment. Over time, such vocalizations evolved to become more nuanced and specific. After the leopard, the danger was an eagle, then a snake. Then, sitting around a warming fire, the early hominids reminisce about what happened. Such reminiscences are stories told to family, tribes, and larger social groups, which lead to identity and bonding. This is the way the naturalist, the evolutionary biology student, the Daoist in me, sees a story. As a way of better understanding and sharing the lessons of nature—including human nature: without a message, language has no purpose.

Flower City Publishing in Guangzhou, a Chinese publisher with a sterling reputation, becomes interested in my work. We make a deal to translate and publish a trio of my books, starting with *YIN: A Love Story*. I travel to meet their team, and I find them to be smart and innovative. I like that they see our work together as East-West bridgebuilding, and that their principle, Xiao Surong, understands and appreciates Daoism and its role in Chinese culture and we exchange ideas over an amazing vegan Chinese meal.

> I think Daoism can save the world, but how did a New Yorker like you come to know about it and be interested in China?

> Actually, I don't understand why everyone isn't more interested in China. What's so compelling about America other than commercialism and a big military? The founding experiment seems rebellious and cool and some of the music is great, but if you look closely, you see America was founded on a desire not to pay taxes and to have our own religion be the dominant one. We went on to commit genocide on our continent's native population, then build an economy on slavery with unbridled greed and materialism. To this day, we're as economically stratified as China is, but with a far thinner culture. Of course, that's forgivable as we're such a young country and America has great potential and fantastic natural resources, and I'm constantly grateful for my own freedoms and education and advantages. Still, objectively speaking, we could do a lot better. We still have not yet figured out the proper distribution of wealth, for instance, or how to be tolerant of other religions and races. We are far ahead of China on human rights and the checks and balances against totalitarianism, but even so I am constantly entranced by all the stories I find in China's history.

In 2016, I'm on an airplane from New York to Florida. I have a first-row seat, luck of the draw as there are only economy seats, and nobody is sitting next to me. I look forward to having a little elbow room and some time to read a book

THE PATH FINALLY CLEAR

I have brought along. At the last moment, just as the door is closing, a woman rushes aboard. She is all Palm Beach, wrapped in furs and designer clothing, dripping with jewelry and enough cologne to cover the elephant house at the zoo. She slides into the window seat beside me and pulls out an e-book reader. We take off. Half an hour in, she turns to me and gestures at an old Omega I wear mostly because it reminds me of Master Pan, who has the same old watch.

> *I like your wristwatch.*
>
> *Good to know.*
>
> *A man like you really needs a nice watch.*
>
> *A man like me?*
>
> *Just so people don't take you for homeless.*
>
> *Homeless? Really? Sitting next to you on an airplane?*
>
> *I'm in the fashion business. I mean because of the yoga clothes.*
>
> *Thanks for the sartorial consult.*

I go back to reading.

> *What do you do, anyway?*

I close my book and hand her a business card.

> *You're a monk? Oh my God, I'm such an idiot.*

She brings up a web browser on her iPad and starts reading about me.

> *You're not just a monk, you're a famous monk!*
>
> *But all these books.*
>
> *I write books. Lots of people do.*

She seems very excited.

I have this friend, Yue Sai Kan. She's like the Oprah Winfrey of China. You have to meet her.

I'd be happy to.

Right there and then, she sends Yue Sai a text, and by the end of the flight, China's Oprah and I have agreed to meet the next time I'm in New York.

A few months later, I stand in front of Yue Sai Kan's beautiful Manhattan brownstone. She has had an amazing career as a TV journalist, documentarian, fashion icon, pageant promoter, and goodwill ambassador for China. She is lovely, gracious, and kind—as we talk, she gets a funny look on her face.

Wait a minute. I know your family! Your father was my doctor! I think I even met you when you were a little boy.

We marvel together at how small the world is. I notice a beautiful tree in her backyard.

Spoken like a true monk. All this expensive art and furnishings, and you notice the tree. What can I do to help you?

I don't need anything. I'm just happy to be here with you.

What about your books? Shouldn't those those wonderful Chinese historical fantasies be turned into films so more people can enjoy your stories?

That would be great.

A few weeks later, she puts me in touch with John Zheng, President of Wanda Pictures, a large and active Beijing production house owned by one of China's premiere real estate magnates. We make an appointment for the next time I'm in China and I send ahead some scripts.

A few months after that, I'm traveling in China with Master Yan. We are in Changsha, Hunan Province, visiting a Daoist temple there. When we are finished, we take a bullet train to Beijing. En route, I'm stunned by the apocalyptic landscape, the vision of people clustered around trashcan fires behind low concrete hovels, the putrid waterways, the brown sky, the utter and complete environmental holocaust unimaginable to and by anyone I know back home. I talk to some young people on the train. They are on their way to the capital, their first trip away from the industrial heartland of north-central China. Their English is far better than my Mandarin and they wax ecstatically about how much they love America, particularly Hollywood movies. I ask them which movies and what they like so much, seeking insight, I suppose, into what they respond to in terms of story, talent, sagas, epics, heroism, mythology, and themes. Instead, they tell me they love the way the movies are painted. I'm confused.

Painted? What do you mean, painted?

Well, we mostly love the way movies show the sky as blue.

In a terribly sad moment, I realize that these kids, affluent enough to afford a highspeed train, have never witnessed a clean sky. Living in a landscape of factories and air laden with heavy metals that refract sunlight into brown and gray, they have only seen particulate filth when looking up.

We arrive in Beijing. Image is important, so I pick a fancy hotel and let the studio know where I'm staying. The next morning, as I dress to go meet John Zheng, I watch BBC News. The anchor no sooner speaks the word China than the screen goes black. I check the cord. I test the lights in the room. It does not immediately occur to me that I have just witnessed censorship in action. I'm about to call the desk to let them know my TV is sick when the screen comes alive again. This time, there is coverage of President Trump taking a call from the President of Taiwan, an action that infuriates China. The news anchor predicts this will have a chilling effect on Chinese/American relations and make business more difficult. Knotting my tie for my Chinese/American business meeting, I scream out loud.

Oh no! Why today? No!!

Master Yan coaches me one last time on Chinese business etiquette as we take the elevator to the top of a Beijing skyscraper. Soon, we are ushered into John Zheng's office. We exchange pleasantries and gifts with him and his head of production, Cary Cheng. I have brought a nice pen and some cigars. In return, I receive some promotional tchotchkes for the company's upcoming film, *The Great Wall* (which will prove to be a tremendous flop). We all sit down, and I outline four different films based on my published and forthcoming novels. The longer I talk, the more obvious it becomes that these men have no real intention of doing business with me. Eventually, Zheng pulls out his phone and starts playing with it.

Sensing that a great opportunity is about to fly out the window, I stand up. Master Yan looks at me with great concern. His expression turns to horror as I begin talking.

Listen to me. My whole life is Chinese culture and history. If you visit my home in America, and I hope someday you will, you will find evidence of this in every corner and on every wall. As a result of this devotion, I have written great stories of China, stories that are of interest to people around the world. Stories are the backbone of all successful novels and films. Without good ones, you won't achieve the critical success you want. Relying on special effects and famous actors, you won't be accepted in the West as I know you wish to be. You need me just as much as I need you.

The silence that follows is deafening. Master Yan covers his face with his hands. Cary Cheng is frozen in place. Zheng stares at me, then licks his lips. Suddenly, looks at Cheng.

He's right you know. Let's do his stories. All of them.

Cheng pulls out a pen and starts making notes.

Which one first?

The one about the jade robot in the court of Kublai Khan.

Right. Incredibly cinematic, that one.

The turtle story after that, then the spear queen story, and finally the one about the admiral who discovered America before Columbus.

Everyone smiles and Cheng asks me a question.

Will you sign a contract now?

I'm delighted to sign, but my New York agent has to review it first.

No problem. I'll be in New York in ten days. I'll meet with him then.

We stand up, shake hands, smile, and leave. Master Yan is quiet until the elevator doors close and we are halfway to the ground floor. Then he suddenly breaks into a huge grin.

You did it. Not if, but definitely; not when, but now.
Congratulations!

I'm so glad he is pleased, and I'm excited about the prospect of working with the film crew. Always ready for an excuse to party, Master Yan selects a typical Beijing restaurant and invites his family. Everyone is excited and we have a great celebratory dinner with toasts and marvelous dishes. I'm already envisioning what these films will do to spread Daoist ideas in the West and to bring a Western sensibility to Chinese history and drama, one that will bring the US and China closer together.

Once we are back in the United States, however, things begin to break down. Cary Cheng does not meet my agent in New York. Communications between me and Wanda begin to thin. At length, Master Yan receives a message intended for me. It says that the company does not see a way to adapt the story about the robot to film. This, of course, is the same story that they were previously so excited about. No mention is made of any of the other works. Master Yan tries to get them to agree to another meeting, but they are vague. I'm greatly disappointed but he reassures me.

Remember how long it took to work out the deal with Flower City Publishing and how long it took to receive your ordination certificate after becoming a monk? You have to be cleared by the government. All these companies are part of the government now.

If they really want to make the film, I can help them with the adaptation. Honestly, doing business in China is like doing business on Mars.

Have you not heard what I just said?

I have. I'm just a stubborn idealist and think everything should be different. I think the work should stand on its own. It seems wrong that the Communist Party should be involved in censoring, approving, or translating novels, not to mention making movies and ordaining monks. Governments work for people, not the other way around. And when it comes to monks, well, there should be a separation of church and state.

Master Yan vigorously shakes his head.

There has never been a time in China when religious institutions were separated from centralized power. There was always a flow from the life of a city official to the freedom of being a recluse in the mountains and a pull against that from government, mostly because rulers wanted to be counseled by masters and to control them. Free thinkers, strong thinkers, respected community leaders, all these pose a threat to tyrants. And no, the government has never, ever worked for the people, despite claiming to do exactly that. Not in China.

The experience with the movie studio makes intensely personal issues that were once foreign, insubstantial, theoretical, exotic, terrible in theory but distant. The rise of tyranny in the world, both at home and abroad, is no longer a matter to cluck at during newscasts. China and America are estranged, as they were always bound to be, and the consequences have become part of the story of this Park Avenue monk. Not only do my book and movie deals evanesce, but relationships I treasure have done so, too. I lose close touch with Master Pan and Master Che as their domestic situation becomes increasingly precarious. I think

233

about Hitler's Holocaust, a multi-generational wound that is ever-present in my family history. I think about Germany in the 1930s, when people kept their mouths shut because it was in their own personal interests to do so, because they did not believe that what was clearly happening could possibly be true.

Watching Donald Trump and Xi Jinping destroy democracy leads me to pen my feelings, and when I share a draft of them, my literary agent exhorts me to drop all other projects and turn those thoughts and feelings into a book; a manifesto that outlines precisely those steps we must take, as individuals and as global societies, to regain the path of compassion toward all sentient beings, frugality in the use of our natural resources, and humility in our dealings with one another. *Mad Monk Manifesto* is released less than a year later in 2018, generating some applause, some criticism, and winning some awards. More importantly, at least to me personally, is the way giving voice to important ideas helps me keep my *wuji*, my equilibrium.

———·———

Aside from the powers of story, there is nothing more grounding and essential to the human brain than the direct, physical experience of moving through the material world. I have been practicing and teaching martial arts for more than forty years now and have been running a tai chi group in South Florida during the last twenty-five. In that time, my students have become my extended family. I'm their *Shifu*, an evocative Chinese term that means a combination of father and teacher, with all the bidirectional responsibilities, affections, and trust such a twin role entail. My students range from elderly folks who study tai chi to improve their balance and avoid morbid falls to teens who want to compete with swords in tournaments. I have a world-renowned policeman as a student, other martial arts teachers, CEOs, physicians, and other wonderful students too numerous to mention. My senior student, Jennifer Beimel, has studied twice per week with me for twenty-three years. She follows me through the evolution of my own practice, learns new skills as I do, and helps me with teaching. My wife, Janelle, studies with me too.

I'm on to a new pursuit in my tai chi training, perhaps the most difficult one yet. It is mastery of the ten-foot military spear that I seek. Why such interest? After all, there is nothing practical in it. I can't carry a spear around for self-defense, and even if I could, the usefulness of such a weapon died the day the gun was born. No, the martial side of Daoist practice, tai chi and related internal Chinese martial arts, was critical to the survival of exponents of practitioners years ago, but today, in the era of Glocks, cruise missiles, and biological weapons, that side is of interest for self-cultivation and what it teaches us about ourselves. Any thinking, awakened person realizes that violence, after all, is the lowest common denominator of human existence. Even for security personnel, soldiers, or policemen, an abiding fascination with it is a sign of an unbalanced mind at the least and mental illness at worst.

Tai chi was once a battlefield art. The battlefield is no longer the plains, mountains, forests, and deserts of China but a world with its own tangible stresses, including the weapons of mass distraction to which we are all unwillingly subjected, the pace required by a constant digital presence, the pressing urge of competition and technology that leaves us all sick enough to fuel a trillion-dollar healthcare industry that does everything but cure us. Balance and harmony are gone—we are destroying the natural world around us by the minute, and we live under the real and constant threat of both global pandemics and global thermonuclear war. Tai chi's ancient moves now help us fight the degenerative diseases of such stresses and, of course, of aging. All Daoist pursuits help still our minds. What we now consider the impractical sides of training are those most likely to be lost, yet without a firm grasp on the art's intended purpose, we cannot be sure we accurately understand it. I therefore take joy in keeping the historical, Daoist dimensions of tai chi alive.

When it comes to the long spear, I want to be able to replicate the feat, attributed to the martial arts legend, (and Bruce Lee's teacher) Ip Man, of pounding a nail into a tree with a single thrust. Fittingly, I'm also inspired to learn this quintessential and most challenging of traditional Chinese weapons by a literary love affair with China's thirteenth century spear queen, Yang Miao Zhen, who I first hear of in the early 2000s when I'm taught the rudiments of her spear-fighting system. I decide in those first few days that I want to write a novel about her, as she is one of the very few women in Chinese history to have become a ruler in her own right and a warrior of such ferocity that she was able to repel the universally feared Mongols and the warriors of the Southern Song Dynasty with equal dispatch. She is the originator of a fighting system so revolutionary and effective that it was employed more than a century later by the legendary Ming dynasty general Qi Jiguang to repel plundering Japanese pirates and later defend the Great Wall.

In *Wasp Warrior* I conjure Miao Zhen as confident, beautiful, and competent beyond measure. I imbue her with charm, power, and omnivorous sexual appetites, which gives me great fodder for my story. I also make her a serial killer. As usual when it comes to writing about ancient China, I employ two parallel storylines, one in the present and one in the past, gradually intertwining the two as the novel progresses. This is the same narrative tactic I employ in *YIN: A Love Story* and in *YANG*, the jade robot novel that so entranced the folks at Wanda Films.

In these and subsequent works, I see that I have finally managed to meld my love of story, of fiction, of writing, with my quest for the underlying truth about life. The manner in which I have combined my artistic urges and my philosophical bent may be Daoist, but it is also mine and mine alone, not a prescription nearly so much as a decoction—a mixing of the twin pursuits of art and spirituality. This makes for a satisfying life, and I would have no other.

There have been so many famous people drifting past me in my life and so many diverse and exotic experiences, too. While meeting these and living those, I have always been mindful of the Daoist saying *da dao wu xing*, which roughly translates as "the Dao is big, so keep your eye on the big picture." I have noticed that with fame comes a lack of balance, and with fortune comes a lack of privacy, center, and often compassionate awareness. I have noticed that a narcissistic preoccupation with individual wants and needs results in frustration, alienation, sadness, and depression for an entire population. I think back to the entertainers who peopled my childhood and see hurting souls desperate for adulation. I think back to the politicians and tycoons and see disconnection and an addiction to power. I also think back to the marvelous few who managed to juggle it all and stay in balance.

Most of the folks who peopled my childhood are gone now. My relationship with my mother is stable, though she is not in robust health, and we spend kind and close time together whenever we can. My father, sadly, has passed and I have come to see his choices and values in a different way than I did as a child. I loved him and I miss him. My relationships with my siblings are solid, though, as is true for almost everyone, nobody has an ideal life and sometimes old patterns emerge. The good news is they are banished quickly and we all share a love of crazy humor and outrageousness and, in the face of both childhood memories and the twists and turns of life, we laugh together a lot.

After the tragedy of my first marriage, my second has proven the gem of gems. I can't imagine anyone but my wife, Janelle, putting up with my esoteric interests and non-mainstream views, my wont to drop what I'm doing and dash off to Asia for training or a writing retreat—not even complaining about taking care of our five dogs and the little group of exotic turtles that live in our laundry room. Nor can I imagine anyone more steadfast, loving, and caring, the yin to my yang and the perfect balance to my eccentric and mercurial personality, all rolled up into a world-class business genius with a meteoric career.

Had I spent years concocting the perfect son to render in a novel, I would have fallen far short of imagining a more compassionate, committed, enthusiastic, artistic, and brilliant man than the one our son, Tasman, has become. From musical talent and riveting oratory to a world-class scientific mind and photographic eyes, it is always a joy to watch him thrive and grow. The time I spend with him these days is as precious as ever and for that I am blessed. I am a child no more, and if I have ever been a victim, I have forgiven those who transgressed against me, seeing the tapestry of which we are all a part and understanding that to hold resentment, judgment, or ill-will in my heart is to damage me more than anyone else. I have tried not to lose perspective and get lost in the speed and greed of Western material life. I have also tried to preserve the deliberate guilelessness and naivety of childhood, loosen the ties that bind me, and empty my mind of as many facts and judgments as possible, all the better to see the world more clearly. Sometimes, during this long journey, I have done these things well. Sometimes, I have done them poorly. Yet sooner or later, no matter how wide the swing of my spiritual pendulum, I always return to the immanent world.

That is why, even though I no longer live in New York, I am still, and will always be, the Monk of Park Avenue.

AFTERWORD

In 2019, I relocated from South Florida to Southern Arizona. A few months after the pandemic hit, I contracted a systemic fungal infection called Valley Fever. This relatively common disease affects thousands of people every year but the powers-that-be in Arizona don't want news of it to affect the state's rating as the number one move-to destination. Some folks clear the fungus on their own. In others, the fungus settles in nodules in the lungs and requires treatment. In others, the disease disseminates to other parts of the body. The worst place it can go is the brain, which makes for a rare but incurable condition that requires a lifetime of strong, daily medication. Regrettably, I contracted that version.

I spent the summer of 2021 in and out of the hospital with various complications. The pain was so intractable much of that time that I frequently contemplated ending my life or asking for it to be ended. In September of that year, I suffered septic shock and was rushed to the hospital. I was conscious long enough for the ER physician to tell me he would do his best to save me but was making no promises. I was very, very sick. I told him I was a Daoist monk and that we have a different view of death than people in the West, seeing it as the natural continuance of life, the yin to life's yang. I told him that if I passed away, he shouldn't let it bother him, as I had wanted to go often during the intense misery of the last year. I only asked him that since Janelle was outside the treatment room, he please spare her hearing me die in agony.

He and his team succeeded in saving me and I spent the following days unconscious in a hospital bed. During that time, I had what I can only describe as a sustained, four-day vision. This vision, this journey, was clearly curated for me and me alone. Who or what the curator was was not clear, but his or her presence was obvious. There was no wish-fulfillment, no Master-Po-like figure, no ancient Chinese landscapes or other expressions of my subconscious wishes or desires. I was being deliberately *shown* things by the curator. I zoomed through cosmos, passing stars, planets, comets, and asteroids. I penetrated galaxies. I saw evolution at work on multiple planets. I saw the future of organic life on Earth as well as the specific future of humankind. I watched everything but that last item with gratitude and equanimity. Humanity's future was one I could not abide. I pushed back and was told, in no uncertain terms.

> *I'm sorry but it doesn't matter what you think. It's not about you. This is the way it is, the way it will be.*

Upon awakening from my journey, I asked Janelle to play "Amazing Grace" on her phone. We listened together to various artists. I focused on the word "wretch" in the lyrics. I felt a wretch because I knew in my heart of hearts that while the monk of my dreams and ambitions would go through anything and everything to achieve the awakened state in which the vision left me, if I were offered a chance for a do-over, an opportunity to avoid the pain and suffering that had brought me here, I would jump on. What's left is that I am consciously in a state of perceiving all-that-is, which is to say the interconnectedness of all things that is at the heart of Daoist thinking. Such realization has come at a tremendous price. I'm not sure anyone gets to this point without the intervention of some outside circumstance or force. It's hard to believe one could find this state merely through intensive meditation. Others disagree and I can only bow to them, for they are better than I am.

Further details of my vision are for me. I don't know that they will ever find their way to print nor even that they should. What I do know is that they have left me convinced of the irrelevance of ego and the importance of compassion and daily service. I find a new commitment to the practical and compassionate teachings of Daoism, primarily for their ability to alleviate suffering and mitigate conflict. I find some small succor in the fact that although my prognosis is uncertain at best and although I have been greatly physically diminished by such a long and serious illness, I could never have survived without all these years of Daoist practice. More, I believe illness has made me a better monk.

February 2, 2022, Tucson, Arizona

DAOISM: A SYNOPSIS

Do I really believe Daoism can save the world? Well, yes, but other people believe that about their belief systems, too. Is it a natural, inborn feature of all religions and philosophies that their adherents see them as humanity's salvation, or at least the answer to many problems? I suppose it is. And I also suppose it to be typical for a follower of a particular belief system to think their way is the only true way. Usually, though, there is a clash between modern understanding of the world and religious beliefs, and there is a clash between those beliefs and the way nature works. Daoism, however, despite its philosophical and religious aspects, also functions as a science. Specifically, it represents the earliest (but still relevant and sophisticated) expression of systems and chaos theory. It also foreshadowed quantum physics and presaged the digital revolution. As if that were not enough, it systematically addressed the way our environment can shape our beliefs and moods—and how those mental states can in turn change our physical bodies—thousands of years before the field of epigenetics was established. In short, the modern scientist (if he or she is motivated by curiosity as opposed to by corporate or government directive) is doing the same work Daoists do when they closely observe nature.

Perhaps this underlying common ground is what allows Daoism to exist as a complement to modern science rather than standing in opposition to it. Like biology, Daoism offers practical directions for living based on how nature works. Like sociology, it provides guidelines for getting along with others. Like psychology, it helps us understand ourselves. Unlike those disciplines, it does all these things coherently. In this way, Daoism anticipated the breaking down of departmental barriers and the emergence of multidisciplinary studies seen in the best universities today.

If I'm to pick one unique aspect of Daoism that strongly differentiates it from Western faiths and philosophies, that would be the absence of man from the center of things. Man is small, not only in traditional Daoist landscape paintings, but in the entire Daoist view of the cosmos. The human being has a singular but diminutive presence and role, suspended as he or she is between Heaven and Earth. In the grand international buffet of religions, therefore, Daoism may be found between the anthropocentric, monotheistic traditions, with their beliefs in a personal God and the importance of sainted interlocutors, and Buddhism, with its emphasis on self-annihilation and the pursuit of freedom from attachments, desires, and the suffering they bring. In some senses then, Daoism gives people a bigger role than Buddhism does, but a far smaller one than do the descendants of Abraham.

I love the fact that Daoists don't believe in any separation between humans and the rest of nature, a loathsome conceit if ever there was one. I love the corollary view that abusing nature is therefore tantamount to abusing ourselves. Indeed, because its seeds sprouted in Neolithic proto-China, a time when men and women lived in necessary and intimate association with nature, Daoism may be the original environmentalism. What a stark contrast it thus offers to the Western notion of humans having hegemony over the natural world after it being gifted by a concocted god! Given this alternative, more rational and accurate interpretation of the world, it should be no surprise that alternative medicine, the self-reliance movement, rewilding, mindfulness, sustainable agriculture, industry without planned obsolescence, human rights, self-care, and the growing awareness of climate change and environmental responsibility are all redolent of ideas Daoists advanced millennia ago.

————·————

Rooted in Neolithic shamanism, Daoism (as we know it now) appeared during the period scholars call the Axial Age—a period of human history during which art, science, spirituality, and academic intellection emerged in force. The putative Daoist sage, Laozi, lived during this time along with his disciple, Confucius. Plato lived in this era, as did the Buddha (Siddhartha Gautama), Zoroaster, and the fathers of Jainism, Parshvanatha and Mahavira. In China, these years bridged the Spring and Autumn, and Warring States periods.

China's intellectual power elite were Daoism's champions, fans of its elegance and practicality. Artists of that time loved it, too, and applied a Daoist view to their paintings, their calligraphy brushstrokes, their poems, even their pottery and castings. Merchants of the day, paragons of practicality who only adopted techniques that made business more profitable, utilized Daoist ideas to increase their efficiency and enhance their ability to see upcoming trends. Daoism fully flowered, however, during China's two most successful and enlightened dynasties: the Han and the Tang—China's golden age.

One possible reason for Daoism's historical success is the key tenet that softness always overcomes hardness. China's entire history might well be considered a series of efforts on the part of civilized agriculturalists to repel nomadic invaders from the north and west, and this Daoist tenet was employed by both China's political leaders and its military generals against these incursions. Thus, the Daoist martial strategies of Sunzi, combined with the allure of the comforts and security of a civilized society, allowed China to seduce invaders, ultimately taking advantage of hybrid vigor to incorporate nomadic bloodlines into Han bloodline and thereby strengthen the population. Unlike ancient traditions that remained stuck inside static, primitive societies—and thus died with them—Daoism has grown richer and more profound with every challenge or threat.

Before the year 142 CE, Daoism was already the philosophy to which I so enthusiastically adhere, namely shamanism with an intellectual twist, a beautiful, elegant synthesis of what wise and patient observers of nature concluded from lives of quiet contemplation. These brilliant minds were not distracted by television, podcasts, radio, or multiplex cinemas, nor by browsing the World Wide Web. Actually, their investigations took them deep into the place where mind becomes body, and thence directly into medicine. Given the friction between medical science and religion today—vaccines, viruses, abortion, stem cells, and more—it is even more ironic that Daoism was turned into a religious movement by a physician, Zhang Daoling, who founded a sect called the Way of the Celestial Masters.

A physician, Master Zhang was successful because his medical prescriptions helped his patients, engendering their loyalty both to him personally and to the ideas he claimed to have received through mystical revelation. Whenever direct mystical experience meet politics—as they eventually do in all religions—conflict and trouble are sure to follow. In Zhang's case, his original group of followers devolved into a series of increasingly individuated sects. Today, religious Daoism exists in pockets across China, at least until the current regime completely destroys it. What does such a religion look like in daily life? Think ceremonies with monks walking and chanting, and people burning paper money in effigy to ancestors, especially during funerals. Think rituals around natural events, changes in season, eclipses, weather, and more. Indeed, Daoism's full expression is so complex, it now demands scholarly treatment in tomes.

At the very least, religious Daoism does something on a local scale that philosophical Daoism does on a global level; it generates a community of likeminded people who have found its tenets practical and usable as both a spiritual system and recipe for living. Using intellection, meditation, and physical practice, Daoists develop calm, clear minds and an abiding sense of the rationally unfathomable fabric of which our world is made. Daoists pursue the so-called Three Treasures—compassion, frugality, and humility. No matter how violent, unpredictable, or treacherous the seas of life may prove, Daoism teaches us to stay cool, calm, and collected. The Daoist word for such a serene state is *wuji*, the same term used to describe a step in the Daoist cosmogony, or creation story. Analogous to the void from which God created Heaven and Earth as chronicled in the Book of Genesis, *wuji* is a state of perfect stillness that is empty yet pregnant with infinite possibility.

When the Greek conqueror Alexander the Great entered the Phrygian capital of Gordium in what is now Turkey, he was presented with a knot so thick and tight, nobody could untangle it. His answer was to slice through it with his blade. Our prejudices, limitations, habits, and beliefs present each of with our own version of that Gordian Knot. We can spend lifetimes wrestling with it, or we can cut through it in one fell stroke, using meditation, *qigong*, or martial practice to return to *wuji* and bring yin and yang into balance. In the state of *wuji*, anything and everything is about to happen, but nothing yet has. To be in *wuji* is to be Master Po.

In the West today, Hollywood superstar George Lucas is, perhaps unwittingly, Daoism's biggest evangelist. His *Star Wars* universe, a fictional rendering of Daoists on a galactic scale, has educated millions in the Daoist Path without ever uttering the word Dao. Lucas renders the historical struggle between Confucianists and Daoists as a conflict between a tyrannical empire bent upon expansion and conquest on one hand and spiritually inclined rebels in search of a just and natural life on the other. In thematic terms, this is the struggle that takes place within both society and the individual, namely the war between narcissism and altruistic compassion, between impulses, gratification, and extremes on the one hand and calm, content, love for all of nature on the other. It is the war between tyranny and freedom, between rules and regulations and a spontaneous, free life.

While Lucas' juxtaposition makes for entertaining cinema, oversimplification seems unavoidable in popular cinema. Actually, *Star Wars'* rendition of the empire and the rebels overstates the moral dichotomy between Confucianism and Daoism, for neither is completely good nor completely bad. Confucianism—with its dismissive treatment of women and draconian emphasis on fixed social class—preserved a deeply authoritarian and unjust social system yet also cohered and preserved Chinese society for 2,500 years. Daoism, while exhorting rulers to keep their subjects in the dark like mushrooms, exalts the sort of meditative reclusion and Bacchanalian revelry that most certainly will not lead to an erasure of poverty, intellectual advancement, the advancement of animal rights, or an exploration of the cosmos. It turns out the two systems work well together, which is why many Confucianists were closet Daoists in China, and vice versa.

Such inclusive and nuanced interplay is the essence of the binary Daoist universe and is symbolized by the *taijitu*, the circular, black and white, yin and yang symbol that these days appears on everything from surf-wear to bumper stickers. While most people see that symbol and think of it as a static representation of opposites, each with a little of the other salted in, it is, in fact, a Chinese pinwheel designed to be viewed in motion; yang in the process of becoming yin, yin in the process of becoming yang. The symbol is a movie, not a still photograph. Even so, yin connotes the feminine, dark, heavy, mysterious, and slow, and yang the male, bright, weightless, obvious, and quick. Historically, the original characters for yin denoted the side of a mountain in shade, while the character for yang depicted the side exposed to the sun.

Daoists don't believe yin can even *exist* without yang, or the other way around, for to be defined by contrast and opposition requires that both opposites be present. In *Star Wars* terms, there would be no rebels (nor their Jedi champions) without an empire, and no imperial fighting forces without anyone to suppress. The way yin and yang change, coexist, change places, and dance together accords with recent discoveries in quantum mechanics, theoretical physics, astronomy, cosmology, and mathematics. More and more, Western scientific inquiry uncovers a fluid, binary model, along with the concept of multiple layers of reality (multiverses) found in early Daoist thought.

The word "Dao" means path or way, though one far subtler and more elusive than a simple hiking trail or road. Like evolution or a divine intelligence, it moves things forward and binds them together but, as I already noted, Dao really is not an "it" at all, being unknowable, omnipresent, and ineffable. Since it is far too abstract to be a deity to which we can speak or pray, or even a process that can be clearly identified through experimentation, I prefer to conjure it simply as Dao rather than "the Dao." Whatever Dao may be, it is everywhere all the time and available to those who diligently seek it. I find it in my everyday life in the West, but also in China, where I visit monks and monasteries as well as Daoist masters. In addition to searching for new information, understanding, and techniques, I make those visits and experience the life of the core community of devotees in places as diverse as the Golden Dragon Temple in Guandong Province (which features a wonderful mushroom-based vegan cuisine) and the storied and politically active White Cloud Temple in Beijing, the de facto head of the original world Daoist organization. In all these wanderings, I attempt the free and easy wandering all Daoists seek, cleaving to no particular timetable and attaching to no particular outcome or agenda.

Such wandering, indeed the effortless way of life known as *wu wei,* is espoused in the *Daodejing,* the gorgeous and infuriatingly abstruse little book I have been reading since I was twelve years old. Said to be the second most widely translated book in the world after the Judeo-Christian Bible, the *Daodejing* is in any case a hugely popular work. Short, opaque, and profound, it was written to either be read aloud as poetry or given voice as song. Five thousand words are divided into eighty-one short stanzas that detail a balanced and sustainable life in veneration of nature and her laws. Its author is said to have served as a wizard or fortuneteller to a king of the Eastern Zhou dynasty, and a librarian and polyglot able to read countless languages. He is also rumored to have been born old and gotten younger with each passing day, and to have written his famous book while held up at the gate to western territories following his resignation after as much as a century of royal service.

In the same way historians debate the historicity of Jesus, Moses, and other legendary religious characters, they debate the existence of Laozi. Was he a real master or simply a character in a novel, a literary device designed to embody virtue and wisdom and compassion in a way that inspires us? My late friend, the China scholar Guy Leekley, suggested that the *Daodejing* was likely penned by a tea klatch of five or six rebellious Daoist activists of the fifth century BCE in response to the rise of rigid Confucianism. Leekley and others have suggested that such writers attributed the work to Laozi (the name means Old Boy or the Old Master) because of the pervasive current of ancestor worship in Chinese culture. Such an attribution simply gave the work more *gravitas.*

One way to see the *Daodejing* (Tao Te Ching) is as a guidebook for a ruler on how to keep his subjects safe and happy. Another way to see it is as a commentary on the *Yijing* (I-Ching), an older work of philosophy that is often used as a divinatory oracle, though it is also a catalog of all cycles, trends, proclivities, and possibilities in the natural world. If the *Daodejing is* such a commentary, its purpose is to apply the broad lessons nature teaches to the human condition and human affairs. The book makes clear that the only person you can control is yourself, and that the best course is to keep your head down, shun fame and praise, get the job done, and go home. The *Daodejing* repeatedly reminds the reader that compassion, frugality, humility, harmony, and balance are the foundations of an efficient and effective life.

Because Dao is both limitless and undefinable, Laozi begins his great work by saying that the Dao that can be spoken is not the real thing. All we can really glean is that it is omnipresent and everlasting, precisely the thing that leads us to the very first step in any spiritual enterprise, namely the recognition that *something is going on*. Perhaps Dao is an emergent quality of the universe or multiverses, popping out from nature the way Athena popped from Hera's head, replete with a keen sense of cycles and manifestations, and for some people, deities embodied by rivers, streams, waterfalls, lakes, herbs, trees, clouds, and more.

If we accept that definition, then we can say the same about the philosophy we call Daoism, namely that it arises spontaneously as a philosophy when we simply stand quietly and observe nature closely for a long enough period. This awareness of something larger than ourselves has inspired countless cultural creatives, statesmen, and thinkers, and has done so across the ages and across the globe. In cultivating such awareness and pointing at the larger thing in a pure, unvarnished fashion devoid of faith, superstition, and the need for the supernatural, Daoism offers a truly revolutionary way of looking at the world. It is not for the faint of heart nor suited to those who cleave to the status quo and fear a loss of bearings. Daoism is courageous stuff. It is revolutionary. It is subversive. It is incendiary.

All the more so because it is true.

Acknowledgements

I am perpetually grateful to my wife, Janelle, for her steadfast love, support, loyalty, understanding, and ability to keep me from floating off like the soft cloud I inarguably am. Thanks also to my dear and lifelong friend, Peter Meyer, for exhorting me to pen this book and to my friend, the always-deeply-thoughtful Tom Peek, for his sage counsel along the way. Ditto my lifelong friend, Judi Farkas, whose insights never fail to impress me. Master Yan, the bulwark of my adult life, has given me everything. Without him there would be no *Monk of Park Avenue*, in all the senses that statement implies. Thanks to my senior disciples: Jennifer Beimel, Grant Clyman, Nelson Reyes, and Nancy Bautista for their love and support during my long, recent illness, and to the thousands of students who have, over the years and through their own transformations, illuminated my life and given me purpose. Thanks for the community of fellow martial artists, particularly tai chi players, who have provided such great challenges and companionship over the years. I'm grateful for the folks at Mango Publishing, in particular Brenda Knight for her unwavering support no matter how far afield my writing takes me, to Yaddyra Peralta for her perspicacious editing, and to Robin Miller for unfailingly rescuing me from the black holes Microsoft Word can use to entrap a writer. Last but not least, thanks to Dr. John Galgiani at the University of Arizona's Valley Fever Center for Excellence for keeping me alive to write this book.

Photo Credit: Angela Alvarez

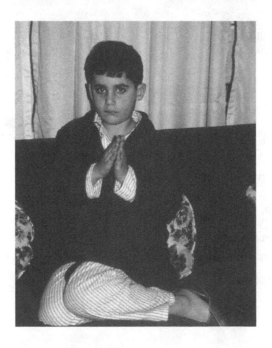

About the Author

Called the new Alan Watts for his teachings and the Zen Gabriel Garcia Marquez for his writings, Daoist Monk Yun Rou (formerly Arthur Rosenfeld) received his academic education at Yale, Cornell, and the University of California, and was ordained a monk in an official, government-sanctioned ceremony at the Chun Yang Daoist Temple in Guangzhou, China. His work has appeared in *Vogue, Vanity Fair, Parade, Newsweek, The Wall Street Journal, WebMD, Fox Business News*, and numerous other websites and newspapers.

His more than twenty award-winning nonfiction books and novels of magical realism focus on philosophy, history, compassion, and culture. From 2010 to 2013, he hosted the hit (reaching sixty million households) national public television show *Longevity Tai Chi with Arthur Rosenfeld*. The American Heart Association profiled Yun Rou as an inspirational resource in 2016.

Monk Yun Rou began his formal martial arts training in 1980 and has studied with some of China's top Chen-style tai chi grandmasters. In 2011, he was named Media Master of The Year at the World Congress on Qigong and Traditional Chinese Medicine. In July 2014, Yun Rou joined the heads of the five tai chi families on the dais, representing American tai chi at the International Tai Chi Symposium in Louisville, Kentucky. He teaches in Southern Arizona, South Florida, and around the world.

Mango Publishing, established in 2014, publishes an eclectic list of books by diverse authors—both new and established voices—on topics ranging from business, personal growth, women's empowerment, LGBTQ studies, health, and spirituality to history, popular culture, time management, decluttering, lifestyle, mental wellness, aging, and sustainable living. We were recently named 2019 and 2020's #1 fastest-growing independent publisher by *Publishers Weekly*. Our success is driven by our main goal, which is to publish high-quality books that will entertain readers as well as make a positive difference in their lives.

Our readers are our most important resource; we value your input, suggestions, and ideas. We'd love to hear from you—after all, we are publishing books for you!

Please stay in touch with us and follow us at:

Facebook: Mango Publishing
Twitter: @MangoPublishing
Instagram: @MangoPublishing
LinkedIn: Mango Publishing
Pinterest: Mango Publishing
Newsletter: mangopublishinggroup.com/newsletter

Join us on Mango's journey to reinvent publishing, one book at a time.